T0289583

THE SCIENCE OF

HOW TO BUILD CONFIDENCE,

PERSONAL

CREATE SUCCESS, AND OBTAIN FREEDOM

POWER

CHRIS LIPP

WILEY

Published by John Wiley & Sons, Inc., Hoboken, New Jersey.
Published simultaneously in Canada.

For general information on our other products and services or for technical support, please contact our Customer Care Department within the United States at (800) 762-2974, outside the United States at (317) 572-3993 or fax (317) 572-4002.

Wiley also publishes its books in a variety of electronic formats. Some content that appears in print may not be available in electronic formats. For more information about Wiley products, visit our web site at www.wiley.com.

Library of Congress Cataloging-in-Publication Data

Names: Lipp, Chris, author.
Title: the science of personal power : how to build confidence, create success, and obtain freedom / Chris Lipp.
Description: Hoboken, New Jersey : Wiley, [2025] | Includes index.
Identifiers: LCCN 2024015729 (print) | LCCN 2024015730 (ebook) | ISBN 9781394273645 (hardback) | ISBN 9781394273669 (adobe pdf) | ISBN 9781394273652 (epub)
Subjects: LCSH: Self-actualization (Psychology) | Success.
Classification: LCC BF637.S4 L5658 2025 (print) | LCC BF637.S4 (ebook) | DDC 158.1—dc23/eng/20240502
LC record available at https://lccn.loc.gov/2024015729
LC ebook record available at https://lccn.loc.gov/2024015730

Cover Design: Wiley

SKY10085501_091924

To JD Schramm,

my mentor and friend

Contents

PART

I

The Roots

1 | See the Water

The CEO's feedback on my latest project was true to his nature – "this is utter (obscenity)." The project would go on to be a huge success. But the boss was the alpha dog. He wanted everyone to know who was in charge, and he did this by pushing everyone down. I walked back to my office, passing a VP in the company. She was fraying around the edges. It wasn't the healthiest workplace.

Every morning I entered the office with the thought, "Why am I not as rich as Mark Zuckerberg? I need to work harder." I had ludicrous self-standards back then. Perhaps that was why I accepted the brunt of the CEO's bullying – I saw it as a step along my career path, and the money wasn't bad. But the stress was building. I suffered stomach pains and backaches. I sought out physical and mental therapy. Eventually I turned to more primal coping mechanisms. When I used the office restroom, I'd write the CEO's name on a sticky-note, toss it in the toilet, and relieve myself over it. That helped.

The CEO's behavior was contagious. One afternoon I watched an employee wave his hand at his colleague and call him "stupid" with such condescension that I thought it deserved an Academy Award. The other employee had the wherewithal to

3

stay calm and explain his ideas, although I had no idea how. I took the scene in stride because it wasn't unique. My manager left the company shortly after, replaced by a friend of the CEO and one of the sleaziest people I ever knew. He bragged about the crazy things he'd done in racecars, the money he dropped on glitzy entertainment. Ironically, he was eventually fired by the CEO as well.

Perhaps the pivotal moment for me occurred after I participated in a speech contest. That was how I spent my free time back then. One thousand people competed, and a handful of us made it to the final round. I won the contest. I shared the news with my team the following Monday. Word must have gotten around because when I met with the CEO later that day, he casually mentioned that his cofounder was the best public speaker in the company. He made pointed eye-contact to see whether I would challenge him. Instead, I decided it was time to pack my bags and move on.

The CEO wielded his authority like an iron fist and purposely disempowered his employees. This was a very clear power dynamic. Had I understood power back then, I might have been able to protect myself and reduce my stress. But if anything, I rejected power because of the way I saw it used. I had no desire to act like that CEO. What I did not see were the many ways other powerful people behaved.

Take Pat Gelsinger, the CEO of Intel.[1] Pat literally started from the bottom of the Intel hierarchy as a technician. It's a straight forward role that doesn't require a college degree. Pat earned his degree while employed and worked his way into leading the design team for the 486 microprocessor. Then he became the youngest Intel VP at 32 years old. How did he do that?

What's fascinating about Pat is that he's a strong Christian and intensely focused on the values of his faith. This means that his modus operandi is not alpha dog. Pat's values include generosity and serving others. He is often invited to mentor employees, a task which he gladly accepts. Pat inspires a high level of trust.

There are few greater successes than rising from the bottom of a hierarchy at a multi-billion-dollar company to the very top. That is exactly what Pat did. Pat's behavior appears to be the polar opposite of the CEO I worked with, and this is what makes the discussion of power so confusing.

When many of us hear the word power, we associate it with power over others. We think of bullies, dominators, and those who enjoy flaunting their authority. We think about the Harvey Weinsteins of the world, the powerful executives who lead organizations with a whip. Power equals being the alpha dog. And there are many cases where intimidation created exceptional results. Andy Grove, another Intel CEO prior to Pat, had the catchphrase "only the paranoid survive."[2] Sounds like a fun place to work, right? When employees shared ideas Andy didn't like, he shouted them down and berated them in front of others. Andy also took Intel's market capitalization from $4 billion to $197 billion during his tenure. That is unqualified financial success.

Anyone with a shred of ambition wants to get ahead. Power is the primary vehicle to that end. But it leaves an unpleasant aftertaste in the mind. Mixed in with the possibility of success is a shadow of discomfort. The desire to be strong colliding with the desire to be good. We win on the outside, but we lose on the inside. So instead many of us seek ways to level up on the inside. We learn to be joyful and happy. But joy and happiness do not magically lead to results. We feel great on the inside, but we are still stuck in our jobs on the outside. We spend nearly a third of our lives working. Work is how we support our family. Work is our self-expression in the world. Wouldn't it be nice if we could win on both the inside and the outside?

The result of this conflict has led to the exploration of empathic power, of servant leadership. Herb Kelleher, the CEO of Southwest Airlines, is a shining exemplar of this approach. "I'd rather have a company bound by love than a company bound by fear," said Herb.[3] He arm-wrestled colleagues and asked employees about their families.[4] Not too different in some respects to Pat Gelsinger. Herb not only grew Southwest Airlines to a major airline competitor, but he maintained consistent profits in an industry where every other company went through ups and downs. Just like Andy Grove, Herb was an unqualified success.

On the surface then, there appears to be a contradiction of what it means to be powerful. At the very least, we see two different types of power. On one hand, we have power through intimidation. Alpha-dog power and the desire to dominate. On the other hand, we have power through connection. Collaborative power that honors others. A conundrum only until we understand the truth, which is that these are not two different types of power. There is only one type of power here expressed in two different ways.

The challenge with trying to understand power is that we view it as a set of behaviors. A great deal of research has gone into observing how powerful people act. Some leaders act dominant and some leaders act sensitive. So we make categories – dominant power, sensitive power, and so on. But if power is a set of behaviors, how can the behaviors be so different? Viewing power as a set of behaviors also contradicts our common sense. We all know empathizers and dominators who are weak.

A colleague of mine went to lunch with a group of friends, the youngest of whom was the star basketball player at the local university. Mr. Basketball stood easily 6'7" and was all about "power." In fact, he had just finished reading a book on getting what you want through intimidation. As if he needed it. When the group arrived at the restaurant, the lunch line was out the door. Mr. Basketball ignored everyone and strode to the front of the line. He cut in front of the person there and demanded a table, much to the embarrassment of his friends. The maître d' was about to politely engage when an elderly lady in line spoke up curtly, "Young man, what do you think you're doing?" Everyone turned to stare. Abashed by her words and facing the onslaught of negative attention, Mr. Basketball slunk to the back of the line. Nobody mistook his behavior for power.

We've all seen someone take action that wins our respect. Likewise, we've all seen someone emulate those same behaviors but only convey insecurity and garner disrespect. Power is not something purely external. There is something else going on underneath that we attribute to the person. A powerful person will walk into a room and own it. They radiate an aura that is larger than life. It's not a quality that is easily emulated.

Logically the solution is to associate power with an internal trait like personality. Nelson Mandela is an exceptional example because he maintained his internal power despite being imprisoned for nearly thirty years. All his external power was eliminated. And yet almost overnight Mandela went from being a prisoner to being the President of South Africa. There was something about the man himself.

Many studies have explored the relationship between power and personality. Cameron Anderson and his colleagues at UC Berkeley measured the personality of seventy-four dormitory students to figure out whether personality influenced social status on the dormitory floor.[5] The students were a mix of freshman and sophomores, most of whom had come together for the first time at the beginning of the academic year. Cameron measured personality using the Big Five test, arguably the most famous personality test in the field of psychology. The Big Five measures Extraversion, Agreeableness, Neuroticism, Conscientiousness, and Openness. Cameron then measured the status of each student by gathering peer ratings at two weeks into the start of the semester and four months later at the end of the semester.

The first interesting finding from Cameron's research was the impact of Agreeableness. Agreeableness is about being kind, friendly, and polite to others. Agreeableness had zero correlation to status. Zero. Power is not about being kind, friendly, nor polite. To be clear, power is not about being cold and hostile either. There is no connection between power and hostility, otherwise we would see a negative correlation with Agreeableness. Power simply has nothing to do with kindness nor coldness. You can be a Pat Gelsinger or an Andy Grove and still be the CEO of Intel. These traits don't matter.*

Cameron's results showed that only Extraversion played a significant role in status across both men and women. Extraversion measures "sociability, activity, assertiveness, and positive emotionality."[6] Extraverts generally achieved more status in Cameron's research. That's a compelling finding. Nelson Mandela is commonly viewed as an extravert. But this finding is only a correlation, meaning it's far from the rule. Bill Gates is an introvert. So are Warren Buffett and Rosa Parks.[7] And we all know Extraversion is not a guarantee that someone is powerful. You might be extraverted and yet you don't feel powerful. Understanding that Extraversion has a correlation to status puts us no closer to understanding power because it does not explain why Extraversion is sometimes powerful and sometimes not.

We are now stuck in how to understand power. If we look at behavior, the myriad styles of powerful people provide contradictory results. Power is not something that is simply external. But we are no better off measuring an internal trait like personality. There is no clear trait we can point to that consistently tells us who is powerful and who is not. Power is neither something we can easily emulate nor is power a trait that some people have and some don't. The good news is that while the former may feel frustrating, the latter is most certainly an opportunity.

---

*This was true of both men and women. Do not get caught in the myth that you must lead with likeability. Your power to influence others is not through being liked, as you will discover in this book.

The key to understanding power came from a breakthrough analysis published by researchers from UC Berkeley and Stanford University.[8] This analysis set the foundation for the idea of personal power. Personal power is our perceived ability to influence the world. Unlike formal power, which focuses on external acquisitions such as money and resources, personal power is how we feel about our own capability to create impact.[9] How we feel about ourselves is how we show up. When we feel big, we show up big. And when we show up big, we change the world. Personal power is an inward experience that radiates outward, influencing our feelings, our behaviors, and ultimately the way others see us.

Although intangible like emotions, personal power has a very real impact on our lives. Joris Lammers and his colleagues invited undergraduate students to take part in mock interviews for entrance into business school.[10] The interviews were part of an experiment, but they were conducted by expert interviewers who evaluated students as if they were real candidates. Before entering the interview, Joris was able to subtly influence some of the students to feel a greater sense of personal power in themselves. We will explore how he did this later. Those who went into the interview radiating power were on average 81% more likely to be accepted into the program. These results had nothing to do with interview skills nor building a better resume. Radiating personal power nearly doubled the chance that students succeeded in the interview. I have never encountered a single force that has a greater and more rapid impact on success than personal power.

Aside from the outward success, personal power is a panacea for our inward mental and emotional health.[11] Those who experience higher personal power have greater self-esteem and resilience. Power fosters creativity. Power helps us feel more authentic and believe in ourselves. Power even buffers us from physical stress. In one unique experiment, researchers observed that people who felt powerful were able to keep their hands submerged in ice-cold water longer and with less physical reaction than everyone else.[11] Personal power makes us both figuratively and literally stronger. We show up big.

Conversely, disempowerment causes an almost incalculable cost in our everyday lives.[12] We show up small. Those who experience low personal power are more often the victims of bullying and violence. They negotiate worse outcomes in business. Inwardly, people who experience low power feel greater anxiety and depression. Low power impairs our mental functioning and makes us more prone to choke under pressure.

Personal power is such a basic psychological need that people who lack personal power are driven to restore it by whatever means possible. Those who feel powerless are more likely to buy designer clothing that display expensive brand logos in order to reaffirm their status.*[,13] The powerless turn to addictions or chronic gambling to experience the next win.[12] Some individuals even turn to violence. Ironically, it's often the behaviors of those who feel powerless on the inside that model the worst associations we have with power on the outside.

Truly powerful people are those we respect regardless of their personality. We feel their presence when they walk into a room. We trust them to guide us through challenges. We honor their strength and capability, and we admire their self-drive. Powerful people do not depend on the outside world, they themselves are a source of power that radiates out and energizes those around them. After nearly two decades examining research in psychology, I am convinced that personal power is the most important social concept of our lives. But where does personal power

---

*This is particularly tragic given that people in lower economic status often experience less personal power and are therefore more prone to spend money on expensive brand luxury goods they cannot afford. Conversely, high power consumers are more likely to spend money on high-quality goods and performance rather than displays of status.

come from? And how does our power radiate out so that we show up big?

The Aura of Power

After writing *The Startup Pitch*, which outlines the de facto formula for raising investment, I coached entrepreneurs to secure hundreds of millions of dollars in funding. I sat in investor meetings and watched these pitches take place many times exactly as planned – great structure, great words, great results. But occasionally even perfect words and stellar delivery led to lackluster outcomes. Honestly, I couldn't explain it back then. There was simply a feeling in the room. If you watch *Shark Tank*, you've observed this invisible dynamic. Sometimes investors drool over a startup and compete with each other to invest, other times investors are critical or disinterested despite the great product.

How is it that sometimes when we speak we own the room but other times when we speak nobody takes us seriously?

To understand how we radiate power, I turned to popular books on the subject. Many books on power offer long-term strategies that help us get ahead in the professional world. But these strategies don't play out easily in daily situations. Few if any of these books focus on conveying power through conversation. We relate most frequently to each other through language. Some great books cover body language. Imagine you strategically maneuver yourself onto a high-visibility project. You step into a meeting and strike your power pose. But when you open your mouth, what do you say? And when someone inevitably challenges you, how do you respond? I am a big proponent of executive posture and presence, but no perfect posture is going to protect your power once you start speaking. Language conveys our power to those listening.

But what language conveys personal power? Watching startups pitch, I found that clarity, storytelling, engagement, and all the traditional ways we think about communication aren't necessarily powerful. These skills are effective at conveying messages, but not at conveying power. If traditional communication conveyed power, it would make more sense for future executives to get a degree in communication than business. Persuasion is certainly powerful. My book, *Magnetic: How Great Leaders Persuade and Inspire,* covers a model of persuasion used by leaders, politicians, and the like. But persuasion is not nearly enough. To explore the elusive language of power, I combed through decades of modern psychology research. Combined with my background coaching startup founders and corporate leadership, a tapestry of the language of power emerged.

Power is happening around us all the time. Our personal power is the invisible currency that guides our relationships at work and at home. We experience power among both friends and strangers. We feel it in our community and on spiritual retreat. Power is like water to a fish, we can't divorce ourselves from it. Underlying every social interaction is a power dynamic. Communication augments this dynamic. Before I understood personal power, I could only accept for unknown reasons that I sometimes showed up big and sometimes showed up small. When I began to understand the psychology that created those feelings and the language that radiated those feelings, I was able to deliberately shift my thoughts and words to show up big.

We are a nation of strivers who honor the American Dream and idolize success, and yet today we feel disengaged from work in record numbers.[14] It's mind-bending that our desire for achievement is so disconnected from our professional life. And the reason is we're exhausted. We're disillusioned. We feel our opinions don't matter and our prospects for growth are limited. Simply put, we lack power. And it hurts. If we don't consciously understand the relationship between our psychology and our power, we remain powerless to change it. We cannot see the power dynamic at play between ourselves and others.

Often we wait for someone else to empower us. We turn to our manager. We cajole our colleagues. We await organizational change. Today many organizations aim to create equitable and inclusive environments. But waiting for organizational change only places our power into the hands of others.

If you want to have an impact on the world and support the people you love, you must take the responsibility to empower yourself. You have power, whether you believe it or not. Nobody can force you to feel powerful or powerless, it is a way of being that comes from you. With the right practices, you can develop your personal power without waiting for the world to change and without the need to dominate others. You can become great.

As you read this book, the goal of this journey is for you to become aware of your personal power and be able to harness your language and behavior deliberately to convey that power. Personal power is fundamental to both your inner experience of life and outer behavior. When you understand personal power, you can take control of your life in a way that you always felt was possible but never understood before. The invisible force becomes visible.

2 | Practice Courage

Roone Arledge was furious. He burst into the conference room where his staff waited. Everyone flinched. It was early morning and ABC Sports had just missed broadcasting a world record for the mile at a track event. What kind of sports network misses broadcasting a world record? Roone strode to the center table and threw himself into a chair. He seared his gaze across those present.

The head of ABC Sports, Roone was a perfectionist. Everyone wanted to please Roone, some out of inspiration but most out of fear. Back in the 1970s, sports broadcasting consisted of setting up cameras at a distance from the field to record the action. It was a dry affair with little engagement. Roone came in with an entirely new vision to transport the viewer to the game. He brought in close-up cameras that put the viewer directly into the action. He introduced instant replays. One of Roone's most famous creations was Monday Night Football.

Roone also viewed his work as more important than the people he worked with. When employees underperformed, he tore into them. If the setup didn't meet his exacting standards, he forced everyone to work through the night redoing the production.

In the early-morning meeting, Roone launched into a scathing rebuke for missing the world-record event. The force of his words rattled the window shades. You can imagine how everyone in that room felt. Here was a lion on the lookout for its next kill. The scent of blood hung in the air. Roone demanded to know who was at fault for missing the world record.

There's an old adage about getting ahead in life – associate yourself with wins and distance yourself from failures. No one made eye contact with Roone. Some senior staff turned to face away. The room swelled with silence. Then from the furthest corner, a single hand rose up. The hand belonged to a junior 20-something-year-old boy responsible for securing broadcasting rights. The boy's name was Bob Iger, the future CEO of The Walt Disney Company.[1]

Own Up

If success is about associating with wins and distancing from failures, why did Bob Iger take the blame for missing the world record? And how did Roone react? My first thought was that Bob had strong morals. In America we're taught the story of George Washington. When George was no more than six years old, he received a hatchet as a gift. Little George promptly used the hatchet to cut down his father's cherry tree. After his father confronted him, George confessed that he cut down the tree. His father was proud of George for his honesty.[2]

Many children grow up with the belief that if we're good, we'll be rewarded just as George Washington was rewarded with his father's pride. We take this mindset into business where we expect our good deeds to promote us to powerful positions. But if we're truly honest, few of us associate power with being good little boys and girls. Often we hear idioms about power such as *the weak are meat; the strong do eat.* The path to power is a Machiavellian climb that shuns morality and crushes those in the way. But reputation matters. In a world that depends on collaboration, no one trusts self-serving egotists. Neither the illusion of gain through goodness nor the screw-your-neighbor ethos offers us insight into personal power.

To understand personal power, first we must explore how powerful people relate to the world. What is their power rooted in? Only by understanding the roots can we understand the fruit. This led me to my first counterintuitive discovery.

Let's say you manage a team of employees and your company just issued a salary freeze. You can't give anyone on your team a raise. A group of managers explained how each of them would share the news of a hypothetical salary freeze to their teams.[3] Their responses fell into two categories. Some managers attributed the cause of the salary freeze to something external like the environment. For example, some managers blamed a weak consumer market. Other managers attributed the cause to something within their control. For example, some managers said they could have highlighted the team's accomplishments better to senior leadership. Overall, those who blamed the environment dodged the bullet, while those who blamed themselves took the hit.

How would you break the bad news to your subordinates?

Responses from the group were collected, and then a second group of managers was invited to rate the perceived power of the first group's responses. What explanations received the highest ratings? When the data were analyzed, the results were surprising. Managers who attributed the cause of the salary freeze to themselves were rated *more positive* than those who placed the blame on something external. Managers who blamed the freeze on something outside their control were seen as less powerful, were rated as less believable, and ultimately were less liked. These results were replicated in two follow-up studies. For example, when people read a scenario in which two consultants lost a client, the consultant who said they did not work hard enough was rated significantly more powerful than the consultant who blamed the failure on the client's excessive demands. It pays to take the hit.

When we think of someone who holds power, they control people and resources. Their relationship with the world is one in which they have control. This feeling of control is fundamental to personal power. For example, powerful people are more likely to believe they can influence the flip of a coin or the roll of a die, even though these outcomes are pure chance.[4] Voters who feel personal power are more likely to believe their vote counts, whereas voters who lack personal power feel that their vote is irrelevant. Because what happens feels like it's within their control, powerful people take responsibility for the outcome of events. Taking responsibility is the natural response of someone with power. We don't need to have formal power to feel in control. Personal power represents our relationship to the world regardless of whether we have real control or not.

When I sat down to speak with ExxonMobil Vice President Bill Colton, he said that getting promoted at his company requires more than technical competence. The most important quality is responsibility – did that person do what they said they would do, and did they own up to their mistakes? Taking responsibility is common practice among ExxonMobil leadership. The presidents of each division start senior staff presentations with current issues, highlighting the worst things that happened recently. The executives know that to earn the room's respect, they must lead with what they did wrong before they discuss what they did right.

Blaming and making excuses are the opposite behaviors of control. Blame implies a lack of control over the environment, which in turn implies a lack of power. In blaming, blamers acknowledge their impotence over the situation. We lack respect for people who blame not because of their values, but because they subconsciously communicate their lack of control. Dodging the bullet comes at the cost of losing one's power.

Another interesting finding from the salary freeze research is that the higher managers were in the hierarchy, the more negatively they were viewed when blaming. When we're at the bottom of the hierarchy, it's assumed we lack power and so we suffer less consequence when blaming outside forces. But expectations go up for leaders as they rise in status. When we're at the top, the expectation is we are responsible for all that occurs.

Tesla's Model X was the first electric SUV to hit the streets, and the release was a big step forward for the company. The launch was a success, but several mistakes were made, including too many customizable features that slowed deliveries. Elon Musk addressed the launch later, saying "The big mistake we made with the X, *which primarily was my responsibility*, was having way too much complexity right at the beginning. That was very foolish."[5]

After ABC Sports failed to broadcast the world record, Roone Arledge was furious. When Roone demanded to know whose fault it was, Bob Iger raised his hand. As Bob explained it, after he owned up to the mistake that morning, his words were followed by silence. A deep silence during which Roone stared at him. And then . . . the conversation moved on. Afterwards no one could believe Bob took credit for the mistake. But one thing did change. After that morning, Bob said Roone treated him differently. *With more respect.*

Was Roone impressed because Bob was a good honest boy? Of course not. Roone valued results. Bob conveyed that he had the power to deliver them. Bob might have failed in this instance, but by accepting responsibility he conveyed that the failure was within his control to correct.

Part of what contributes to feeling in control is what psychologists call an internal Locus of Control.[6] The Locus of

Control is not about formal control over the world per se, it's about control over ourselves. Those with an internal Locus of Control feel in control of their behavior and free to act as they choose. This feeling is deeply personal and arises internally.

Conversely, those with an external Locus of Control believe that their actions are influenced by the outside world. They see the outcomes of their actions as resulting from external forces such as chance, luck, or the pressure of others. Because those with an external Locus of Control feel what happens is out of their control, they naturally blame. People who blame do not have worse values than those who take responsibility, they simply have a different relationship with the world from the absence of experiencing control. Thus, blaming not only diminishes our personal power in the eyes of others, it diminishes our power in our own eyes because we concede a lack of control over our lives.

There are other ways than blame that people deal with the feeling of not being in control. Sometimes those who feel out of control try to overly-control things. They become dominators or micromanagers. Peter Belmi and Jeff Pfeffer explored how different people react to being reminded of their own mortality.[7] Being reminded of impending and inevitable death can make us feel out of control and bring up anxiety. In order to manage that anxiety, Peter and Jeff observed that men were more likely to manipulate others in order to regain a feeling of control.* In follow-up research, Peter and Jeff found that people with greater personal power felt less anxiety when reminded of death, making them less likely to act out.

———————

*This was only true of men, not women. Researchers test for gender differences as a rule. Nearly all the research on personal power shows no gender differences. The rare exceptions like this will be noted. Personal power is not gender-specific, it is human-centric.

When we are thirsty, we anxiously grasp for water. When we are abundantly hydrated, there is no thirst. The same perspective applies to control. A sense of control is not a need for control. Those who thirst for control are precisely those who feel it the least.*

Although Bob Iger respected Roone Arledge, when Bob reflected back on Roone's capricious use of authority, he said "For all of his immense talent and success, Roone was insecure at heart, and the way he defended against his own insecurity was to foster it in the people around him."[8] Roone was a powerful man. But the degree to which he exaggerated his dominance over others was the degree to which he undermined his own power.

A feeling of control means we feel empowered to shape our world. This is why powerful people are more optimistic about the future and have higher self-esteem. And when others see us communicate a feeling of control through responsibility, they view us as powerful.

Therefore, the first step to personal power is to embrace a feeling of control and take responsibility. Whereas blame implies a lack of power, responsibility is an act of power.

Our feeling of control plays directly into the following roots.

Don't React

By any standard, Rex Tillerson is powerful. As the CEO and chairman of ExxonMobil who later became U.S. Secretary of State, Rex's story represents the quintessential American dream. He started at the bottom of the career ladder as an engineer at

---

*Personal power does not correlate with exploitation and entitlement. Research out of UC Berkeley suggests that "individuals who believe they have power in their relationships with others were less likely to behave in manipulative and deceitful ways."[22]

Exxon, and he scaled that ladder to the very top. Nearly eve-ryone begins at the bottom like Rex, but very few make it to its zenith. It begs the question what qualities did Rex have that helped him rise up the ranks?

When Rex was an executive VP, he met with another executive VP heading up a different division. The room was packed with staff from both divisions. There was always a bit of inter-affiliate warfare between divisions competing for corpo-rate resources, and this meeting was no different. It wasn't long before things got hot.

The other VP was an old-fashioned loud and excitable guy who let's call Brad. Brad launched into a tirade against Rex's strategy. Brad embodied the classic presence of a powerful per-son. His gestures were aggressive. His voice boomed with anger. Even though Brad's words were about strategy, everyone in the room sensed that this was a personal attack on Rex. The situ-ation was made worse by the fact that it took place in front of Rex's entire team. As Brad roared, he repeatedly looked over at Rex. It was almost as if Brad expected to be interrupted. But Rex just sat there staring back at him. Heated minutes passed. Finally Brad finished his invective and glared.

Brad came in loudly, aggressively, and dominantly. Brad played all the "power cards." Literally every head in that room turned toward Rex with the same question in their eyes – how would Rex respond?

Let's turn our attention to research conducted by Gerben Van Kleef and his colleagues in Europe.[9] They wanted to understand how people respond when negotiators showed anger during a negotiation. Gerben and his colleagues theorized that displays of anger by negotiators would lead others to make more con-cessions, and they showed this through a series of experiments. When one negotiator got angry, the other negotiator who was the target of that anger conceded more. Anger was influential.

But there was a twist. In a follow-up experiment, Gerben conditioned the target who faced an angry negotiator to feel either more or less powerful. For example, Gerben did this by giving the target good or bad alternative offers. Gerben wanted to understand how feeling powerful influenced the target's response to anger.

Targets who felt less powerful conceded more to angry opponents. This was in line with expectations. But when targets felt powerful, they did not concede more to angry opponents. The anger had absolutely no effect on the negotiation. Gerben and his colleagues concluded that "low-power negotiators were strongly influenced by their counterpart's emotional state, whereas *high-power negotiators were immune to the other's emotion.*"[10]

Powerful people are internally driven. They stay focused on their inner thoughts, feelings, and goals without becoming distracted by the thoughts and feelings of others. Leaders are not followers. Think of history's most powerful people from Nelson Mandela to Martin Luther King Jr. These icons stayed focused on their inner signals and did not react to the threats and doubts of others. This is why we associate power with pioneers of change.

Conversely, those with less power depend on others to succeed. Employees depend on employers. Suppliers depend on customers. This dependence motivates the powerless to fixate on how others feel in order to win their approval. The powerless become approval-seekers. If powerful people show displeasure, the powerless will alter their behavior to facilitate a more desirable interaction. If powerful people cast negative judgments, the powerless will do everything they can to defend against that judgment. This is why negotiators with less power react more to the angry outbursts of their opponents – they're focused on the feelings of others. Reactiveness is the realm of the powerless.

At ExxonMobil, Brad stood at the front of the room like a mountain. His chest was thrust forward, hard lines of aggression were etched in his face. After finishing his attack, he stared down at Rex Tillerson. Every person turned to see how Rex would respond.

The traditional view on power would conclude that Brad was set to win this conflict hands-down. What could Rex do to counter that public attack and save face? There was a long pause as Rex sat there. The long pause made the silence even more awkward. Then Rex spoke up in a matter-of-fact voice.

"Are you done Brad?"

Rex began to state his disagreements. He proceeded to logically lay out his reasoning. Rex didn't take personal offense. Rex was confident he was right, and he knew getting upset and defensive wasn't going to get a better answer. That's not typically what we associate with power, and yet employees watching shared that Rex's response was, and I quote, *"the coolest move we had ever seen."* Rex went on to own that room.

If Rex had become agitated and defensive by Brad's outburst, it would have signaled that Rex was influenced by his counterpart's emotions. Defensiveness is a reaction. And Rex would have lost power. But Rex did not react, he stayed focused on his own goals. Rex's lack of reaction communicated implicitly to everyone in that room that Brad had no power over him. Brad was relegated to the dog with a bark but no bite.

This doesn't mean being calm and rational is powerful. You can't reduce power to a simple set of behaviors because the expression of power is contextual. To conclude that being calm is powerful is to make the same mistake as concluding that aggression is powerful. Powerful people are often passionate, outspoken, and expressive individuals. But this expression comes from being plugged into one's inner thoughts and feelings, not reacting to the thoughts and feelings of others.

Adam Galinsky ran a series of conformity experiments to see how those with low or high personal power respond to the opinions of others.[11] Adam had participants write about a past experience of feeling powerless or powerful. Writing about past experiences of power has been shown to temporarily shift our personal power. Adam and his colleagues then asked participants to perform a sentence-completion task that was intentionally made to be boring.

Afterwards, Adam gave participants an evaluation sheet to rate how interesting they found the task. The sheet had spaces for multiple participants to share feedback. Half the sheet was already filled out with ratings by other participants. In truth, these ratings were completely made up. Adam and his colleagues wanted to know whether real participants would be influenced by the previous ratings already recorded.

Ratings were measured on a 1–11 scale, with 11 being most interesting. Before the experiment was conducted, Adam and his colleagues measured the baseline interest score for the task. Without any outside influence, people rated the task at 8.56 out of 11. In other words, 8.56 was the average rating people scored without seeing the ratings of other participants.

The fake ratings on the evaluation sheet showed an average of 9.6. After seeing the fake ratings, would people be influenced to rate the task differently or would they rate closer to the baseline of 8.56? Let's take a look at low-power scores first. The average low-power rating was 9.55. Low-power people matched their ratings almost exactly to the fake evaluations of others. It's likely low-power people saw the opinions of others and were compelled to feel the same. This was probably not a conscious adjustment.

And how did high-power participants rate the task after seeing the fake ratings? The average high-power rating was 8.68. This rating was statistically equivalent to the baseline. Powerful people were not influenced by the opinions of others and stayed true to their own experience.

The key here that separates high power from low power is agency.[12] Powerful people act with agency. Agency involves responding to inner signals over external ones. This is why powerful people perform better in negotiations – they stick to their goals and react less to angry outbursts. This is also why we respect the lone voice. We intuit the mindset required to go against the majority. Whereas those with low agency are far more focused on reacting to others.

A past colleague of mine occasionally showed up late to meetings. He would scurry in hunched over and did his best to avoid attention. Later he would apologize and make excuses. I felt genuine pity for him. His being late had nothing to do with the pity I felt, it was his complete submission of self to how others viewed him. He was reacting by trying to remain invisible. He would have been far more powerful had he walked in head high and taken responsibility for being late rather than trying to hide.

Joanna Hoffman has been called Steve Jobs' "work wife."[13] In the early 1980s at Apple, she was one of the few people who stood up to Steve's reality-distorting demands and helped ground the company in realism. As a result of fearlessly voicing her opinions, colleagues at Apple created the Joanna Hoffman Award. The award was given out annually to the employee who stood up to Steve for what they believed. Of course Joanna won the award the first two years in 1981 and 1982. Debi Coleman won the award in 1983. Later Debi reflected that "I had learned you had to stand up for what you believe, which Steve respected. I started getting promoted by him after that."[14]

If you want to be powerful, tune into your internal goals and feelings. Don't react to the opinions of others. Reaction signals weakness. Respond deliberately. Our personal power arises from our relationship with the world. We can demonstrate our power by remaining internally driven no matter where we stand in the group hierarchy. Once we are anchored in ourselves, we are ready to embrace the final root of power.

Just Do It

Houston is home to the largest medical center in the world. With 21 hospitals and the world's top cancer center, millions of patients travel to Houston each year to receive unparalleled healthcare. Alongside the hospitals are many leading academic and medical research institutions. The med center occupies its own district near downtown, several square blocks of high-rise hospital after hospital. The streets between are peppered with doctors and nurses wearing scrubs as they commute to and from work. Jennifer is a pediatric neurologist at one of these hospitals.* An immigrant from the Mediterranean coast, Jenn loves the mess of crowds and has an infectious laugh that fills the room. She also works with young patients combatting life-threatening illnesses. Fighting the illness is one challenge, but dealing with distressed parents can be worse. Anxious parents do everything to attract attention to their kids. Parents often yell and scream at the staff. Because the hospital is in Texas, it's not uncommon for parents to walk in with guns. It's a pressure cooker situation every day, and as the lead neurologist Jenn has to be on top of her game.

When a young girl came in with Mitchell's disease, a disorder that causes burning pain across the body, the girl's parents fueled a firestorm. Her father, a retired military commander with the air of authority, voiced his contempt of the resident doctor who came to treat his daughter. He dismissed the doctor with disgust and demanded someone with more experience. Middle management staff interceded but were also dismissed, leaving Jenn as the last resort. As Jenn walked down the hall toward the patient, she received background on the girl's condition from the

---

*Many stories in this book show dramatic personal encounters, and I have altered the names of those involved.

resident doctor. But when she stepped into the patient's room, she faced pandemonium. The girl was on the bed writhing in pain. Her mother sobbed hysterically in the corner. The father turned to Jenn and began screaming orders. As Jenn approached the bedside, the girl started hyperventilating. Jenn was sure the girl's anxiety was a reaction to her father's shouts. The father only became more agitated, yelling that his daughter couldn't breathe. The situation was out of control.

Jenn crisply turned to the resident doctor and asked for medication that would ease the pain. As the doctor raced out of the room, Jenn ignored the parents and sat down on the bed next to the young patient. She began to gently coach the girl to breathe in slowly, breathe out slowly. Her words had a calming effect. Soon the girl's anxiety and breath were under control. Then Jenn looked the father in the eye and stated exactly what would happen next – she would give the meds to the girl, she would monitor the reaction, and then she would run more tests to continue treating the main condition.

As Jenn spoke, the father stopped shouting to listen. The mother stopped sobbing. The resident doctor returned with the meds, and Jenn delivered them. From this point on, Jenn controlled the room. The parents were mostly silent while the doctors did their job. As the hours progressed and discussions took place between Jenn and the patient's family, something unexpected happened. A bond of trust began to form. What started as an intractable encounter transformed into closeness. For Jenn, this is literally a normal day's work.

Jenn's power in that room did not magically arise because she was the doctor. She had to display her power. To do this, Jenn did not wield an artificial authority or one-up the father. Nor did she focus on being nice to try and win the family's approval. Jenn did exactly what we covered so far – she exerted responsibility over the situation and did not react to the parents' panic. These two factors were important. But she did something even more important to shift the situation.

Adam Galinsky and a team of researchers at Stanford University explored how personal power influences behavior.[15] Adam invited students into his office and conditioned them to feel either a heightened sense of personal power or a lack of it. Then he sat each student down alone in another room and left to get something. Next to the student was a fan blowing straight at their face. The fan was intentionally placed to be annoying. After leaving the room, Adam recorded students using a hidden video camera. He wanted to know whether students would turn off the fan or move it to be less annoying. Results showed that those who felt powerful were more than twice as likely to turn the fan off or move it away compared to those who felt powerless. The powerless simply sat there and suffered.

But what do our actions convey to others? One of Adam's colleagues, Joe Magee at Stanford, conducted a follow-up study where he showed people a video of someone sitting in the room either moving the annoying fan or not moving the fan.[16] Joe found that people rated the fan-mover significantly more powerful than those who sat there and suffered without taking action. When those watching were asked whether the fan-mover could be a supervisor, 57% said yes. But no one rated the fan-sufferer as a supervisor. These fan experiments give us one of the most important insights into power.

Powerful people are fundamentally action oriented. When we feel powerful, we are more likely to act. And when we act, others see us as more powerful.

Our brains have two important systems that control behavior, the Behavioral Approach System (BAS) and the Behavioral

Inhibition System (BIS). Both systems are important to our survival, but the BAS is the source of our power.*[17] The BAS energizes us to act. When you experience control over your environment, the first root of power, you are activated to move forward. The more control you feel, the more action you take. And the more action you take, the more control you feel. No surprise then that the BAS is associated with positive emotions such as happiness. Happiness signals moving toward a desired goal.

We all hear statements such as, *it's better to ask forgiveness than permission.* This advice models the BAS. We move the fan. General George S. Patton was one of the top military commanders of the Allied forces in World War II. Patton's motto in battle was, "Go forward!"[18] During the war, Patton invaded and captured Sicily in 38 days. Shortly after, he invaded mainland Italy and helped topple Mussolini within months. His focus on offense and complete disregard for defense hallmarks the power mindset. Patton argued that an army who dug ditches was already defeated.

Conversely, the BIS inhibits behavior. The BIS leads us to sit silently and avoid risk. When you lack a feeling of control over your environment, you are at the mercy of outside forces. An environment in which you don't have control poses a threat. To avoid these threats, you don't act. It is much safer to hold steady than it is to do something different. The motto of the BIS is, *don't rock the boat.* You don't move the fan out of fear of reprisal, or perhaps you don't even notice you have the power to move the fan. The BIS is associated with negative avoidance-emotions such as fear and anxiety, and it is one reason why people with low personal power feel more stress.

---

*The BAS and BIS make up two of the primary motivation systems in *Reinforcement Sensitivity Theory*, one of the major biological theories of personality.[23] The third and final system is the infamous Fight-Flight-Freeze system. Popular psychology has historically focused on the Fight-Flight-Freeze system, now it is time we turn our focus to the BAS.

After reading the research on action, I began to wonder – if actions are powerful and reactions are weak, and reactions are actions, how do we distinguish between actions and reactions? To explore the answer, I looked deeper into Joe Magee's work at Stanford. In the fan study, those who moved the fan were seen as powerful. But Joe was interested in why fan-movers were seen as powerful. He conducted a follow-up experiment. Before watching the video of someone moving the fan, Joe told watchers that the fan-mover was asked to flip a coin before they entered the room. If the coin came up heads, the person would be required to move an object in the room. Participants were then told the coin came up heads, and to expect the person in the video to move something.

When the person in the video was seen moving the fan as a reaction to a coin flip, they were not rated as powerful. In fact, those who moved the fan because of a coin flip were rated equally low in power to those who did not move the fan at all. Joe concluded that actions are only seen as powerful when they convey a sense of agency. Actions must be perceived as internally driven to convey power, not a reaction to external pressures and constraints.

Now we see why a strictly behavioral model of power can never be accurate. No action is inherently powerful. The power is evaluated according to context. Sure, some behaviors are naturally more indicative of personal power than others, and we'll explore many of these. But ultimately we look beyond the behaviors to understand power. We can be calm or angry, nurturing or stifling, shouting or whispering. There are no hard and fast rules.

When Jenn stepped into that hospital room with her young patient and the aggressive parents, she ignored the noise and dealt directly with the central issue. Her focus on action earned the respect of the patient's parents. Had Jenn reacted to the father's shouting, it would have been the father who appeared powerful, not Jenn, making the parents even more anxious. We want the people we depend on to be powerful so they can help us. The parents needed to know their child would get the best help possible. It was precisely Jenn's internal goal-focused behavior that made the parents feel secure.

If we were to sum up the relationship between action and power, it would simply be that *powerful people act according to their own goals*. Power promotes goal setting and initiates goal-directed action. Power moves people forward. The more powerful a person is, the more they identify with achieving their goals and the more they persist in the face of resistance. Knowledge is not power, action is power.

Domain of the Powerless

Nothing speaks more clearly to powerlessness than the Bystander Effect. When I read the headline of a woman raped on a public train in Pennsylvania in 2021, I was shocked that no one who witnessed the event called 911.[19] It's heart-wrenching. The Bystander Effect was blamed when no one stepped in to stop the public murder of 28-year-old Kitty Genovese in 1964.[20] The Bystander Effect states that people in crowds remain passive bystanders to events. They don't act. Of course, this is not a rule – many times people do help. But the number of times people don't is not insignificant.

One reason we fall victim to the Bystander Effect is because we don't see the situation as our responsibility. We assume someone else will take care of it. After all, it's a public place. Maybe the authorities should be responsible. This act of sloughing off social responsibility happens everywhere. For example, many pro-environmental consumers don't purchase eco-friendly products despite good alternatives. These people believe the responsibility is on the companies and not themselves to protect the environment. No matter how well-intentioned these people's values may be, their beliefs prevent them from having any real impact.

Another reason we fall victim to the Bystander Effect is that we rely on others to assess a situation rather than our own perceptions. When we witness others not helping, we draw the conclusion that the situation must not be an emergency. Our awareness is externally influenced. I recall the story of a man who fell and smashed his head on a metal post in San Francisco on a Saturday night. He laid on the crowded sidewalk unconscious in a small pool of his own blood *for hours*. Crowds simply walked around him. When someone finally called 911, the man was brought to the hospital and passed away shortly after. It was reported that had he arrived at the hospital sooner, his life could have been saved. The science is very clear that when we see others not helping, we ourselves are less likely to help. Had the street in San Francisco with the bleeding man been mostly empty, some passerby might have acted sooner. The crowd probably killed him.

The Bystander Effect thus illustrates the three insidious elements of powerlessness – a lack of taking responsibility, a lack of following internal signals, and ultimately a lack of action. We judge this to be a character flaw in those who do nothing, but it's not about character. All of us think we would act differently in those situations. But our thinking doesn't make it so. Action is tied to personal power. Those bystanders who walked around the bleeding man in San Francisco were not bad people. They were people like you and me. These people were simply disconnected from their own power at a crucial moment. Regardless of what we think we would do in the same situation, if we don't experience our personal power in those moments, we will naturally act as bystanders too.* I imagine that we will also regret those moments for the rest of our lives.**

At the heart of powerlessness is a reaction to anxiety and fear. Powerless people lack a sense of control in the world, and so they feel threatened by external forces. They certainly won't intercede to stop a rapist on a train. To keep themselves safe from potential threats, whether it is an aggressor or a nameless crowd, powerless people tune out their inner signals and tune into the people around them. They become people-pleasers to secure a sense of safety in a world they do not control. This desire for acceptance and safety is one reason powerless people don't act. *Don't rock the boat.* They also withhold their self-expression to avoid being judged. Ironically, it is much easier to know the views of someone in their power because they communicate their views all the time, but the powerless hide their true selves.

To be powerful, we need to practice courage in the face of fear.

Courageous Action

Rick was a captain at one of the top municipal fire departments in the U.S. He'd been there for 12 years. Previously he worked as a combat medic under enemy fire. Rick was the real deal in serving others. When the Fire Chief entered Rick's office and

---

*In one unique study, participants were initially made to feel either high power or low power. Then in the middle of the study, each person was interrupted by someone suddenly screaming out for help and starting to choke in the lab. In actuality, the emergency was contrived. Eighty percent of high-power people went to help the victim, even though it required breaking study protocol, whereas only 35% of those in low power broke protocol to help the victim.[24] Those who did not help listened to the victim continue choking and then go completely silent and unresponsive. This study is reminiscent of the Milgram Experiment.[25]

**Roughly 60% of Americans witness workplace discrimination. How often do you remain a silent bystander in these situations?[26]

handed him a report about a young firefighter recently diag-
nosed with liver disease, Rick was ready to help.

Firefighters who are physically unable to work in the field
are put on office duty until they recover. This young firefighter's
name was Martin. Martin hadn't returned to the office since his
liver diagnosis, so Rick headed over to Martin's home to discuss
the office work. Rick was shocked at what he found. Martin
was confined to a wheelchair. This strapping youth who was the
epitome of a broad-shouldered fireman was now yellow with
jaundice and weighed no more than 90 pounds. Martin was in
no condition to do office duty.

The situation presented a significant problem. The fire
department did not have a work from home policy. The department required everyone show up at the office to prevent firefighters from cheating the system by pretending to work. Since
Martin couldn't come to the office, he would be required to use
sick time. It would take at least three months to find Martin a
new liver and another six months to recover afterwards. Martin
didn't have enough sick time. In a flash, Rick knew exactly how
things would play out. Once Rick reported Martin's condition,
Martin's sick time would kick in. After Martin's sick time ran
out, HR would perform a medical examination. Martin would
be found medically unfit for duty and then discharged. Martin's
career would be over. So would Martin's ability to support
his family.

Rick couldn't let that happen. He looked into his heart
and knew he had to help. That's when Rick decided that he
was going to break the rules. Rick put together a work schedule that Martin could do from home, simple tasks like creating
pamphlets for community outreach. Honestly, Rick didn't think
Martin had the energy to do even these simple tasks. But as
long as a box of pamphlets showed up on Rick's desk every Friday, Rick would sign off that Martin was completing his duties
in the office. The pamphlets began showing up, although they

looked suspiciously like they were written by his colleagues at the fire station. Rick signed off on Martin's work.

From the organization's standpoint, this was borderline fraud. If Rick was caught, Rick's own career would be over. The chance of getting caught was high – if another firefighter reported that Martin wasn't coming to the office, an investigation would be launched and Rick would be caught. If someone else wanted to work from home and claimed favoritism for the way Martin was treated, an investigation would be launched and Rick would be caught. Rick felt the Sword of Damocles hanging over him. His stress went through the roof. He barely slept at night.

One month passed. Nothing. Two months passed. Nothing. Three months passed. Three months not knowing if each day would be the last day Rick walked into his office.

Martin got his liver transplant.

After the operation, there was no way to pretend Martin could still work. From that point on Martin used his sick time to recover. After sick time ran out, he used his vacation time. His body healed. He learned to walk again. And at the very end of using his time off, Martin was healthy enough to come to the office. The three months Rick gave Martin before the operation was the extension Martin needed to stretch the time to recovery.

Rick was never caught. Even if he had been, Rick said he would've had no regrets.

Pauline Schilpzand and her colleagues wanted to understand what causes people like Rick to act with courage.[21] For example, why do some people speak out when they witness abuse despite the potential for blow back? Why do some people act as whistleblowers when they see corporate malfeasance at the risk of being ostracized or fired? Through a broad analysis, Pauline noted that courageous people almost always ask themselves two questions before acting. The first question is, *am I responsible for this?* In every case, the resounding response from those who acted with courage was *yes*. Responsibility sometimes showed up as acknowledging one's formal authority over the situation. But oftentimes responsibility was merely recognizing one possessed the skills and opportunity to do the right thing. In every case, felt responsibility mediated the choice to act. For Rick, responsibility was knowing that he had the capability to protect Martin despite the rules.

The second question courageous people ask themselves is, *should I act?* It's not easy to act when our behavior falls outside the norm or when we face punishment. There's fear there. If we're not anchored in ourselves, we will naturally take the path of least resistance, which is conformity. But courageous people make the decision to act based on an internal assessment of the situation rather than a focus on the external threat. Those who acted courageously often felt a sense of a duty or a moral obligation to act. In every case, people turned inward and responded from their own values rather than outward allowing the environment to guide them. When Rick began signing off on Martin's work, he knew he was breaking the rules and risking his own career. But he knew in his heart it was the right thing to do.

Take responsibility. Tune in. Take action. This is the equation of courage. Courageous action is an expression of personal power. Sometimes we naturally feel courageous, but many times we do not. During these latter times, we can reassert our power and courage by acknowledging responsibility over what occurs, tuning into ourselves, and then taking action.

Feeling Free

Many issues plaguing the world today did not arise from a lack of values, they arose from the lack of personal power. When we feel powerless, we hesitate to act. Conversely, when we feel powerful, we confront issues and are capable of rallying others to overcome them. Our brain is constantly dancing between feeling powerless and feeling powerful, between controlling our expression and expressing our control. This is the human condition. With leaders and lovers, subordinates and strangers. If we want to effect change, we must tune into our power more frequently.

What is the feeling of power? Powerful people don't feel a need to control the world. Nor do they feel a self-centeredness about being better than others. Power is ultimately not a feeling, power is a way of being. But if we were to associate a feeling with power, it would be the feeling of freedom – the freedom to act on our truth. Personal power is our capacity to act on our values. Seen this way, power becomes one of the most important moral virtues of society.

The following chapters show you how personal power radiates outward to influence the world and secure respect. There are six outward practices of personal power, each one covered in one chapter. The first three practices cover how power serves others. The second three practices cover how power asserts oneself. Personal power both gives and takes. Throughout, you will witness courageous acts of individuals in the face of challenge.

We can only support ourselves and others when we tune into our personal power.

The Power of Awareness

You will find exercises throughout this book that are scientifically shown to activate your personal power. The exercises are doorways into your power mindset. But before we look at how to step into your personal power, let's bring awareness to the many places where you may be leaking your personal power today. Below are three exercises to help you identify power leaks, each one focused on one facet of psychology. Spend some time reflecting on each one.

    A. In daily life, how often do you explain your behavior as a result of the situation? For example, if you arrive late to work, do you blame traffic? When you're rushing, do you blame an external deadline? When work is going poorly, do you point to others? When you act bad-mannered, do you excuse your behavior as a result of how others treated you? How often do you attribute your behavior to circumstances seemingly outside your control, and how often do you explain your behavior as a result of choices you made or failed to make? Pay attention to your thoughts and words as you move throughout your day.

    B. How many hours each day do you spend focused on the approval of others? Reflect on where your thoughts are throughout the day. For example, where are your thoughts when you dress for work? When you speak with colleagues or customers? When you work on a project? When you hit the gym? When you talk with strangers in public or with your family at home? As you move throughout your day, note the percentage of time you dedicate to thinking about the approval of others rather than focusing on your own views.

(continued)

(*continued*)

C. What decisions or actions are you procrastinating on taking right now? Think of all the areas in your life where indecision and inaction are the status quo. For example, perhaps there are small areas of discomfort you continue to tolerate that you could easily correct. Perhaps there is a big decision you continue to procrastinate over. Perhaps you witness ongoing behavior from others that negatively affects you or those you love but you have yet to intercede. Reflect on the areas of inaction in your life and list them out.

PART

II Giving

3

Add Value

Ryan entered the opulent room of white marble. Outside the rain rolled down the floor-to-ceiling windows overlooking San Francisco. Twenty stories up, he felt like a lord overseeing a fiefdom. His footsteps echoed off the marble floor as he proceeded to the small meeting table near a row of gold-inlayed bookcases. This was new landscape for a guy who donned leather jackets and rode motorcycles. He was buttressed by his company's CEO and a board member. Their aviation startup was growing and they needed more money to build airplanes. They were there to negotiate the second tranche of a $12 million dollar investment with the main financier. The CEO would do the talking. Ryan was simply along for the ride.

After shaking hands, the investor leaned back and laced his fingers behind his head. A Rolex slipped from under the cuff of a well-tailored suit. This was the investor's home turf. The investor shared the latest news on the industry. His words emanated confidence. His presence filled the room like an aura. Ryan felt a budding sense of wonder. But Ryan's reverie was broken when his CEO interrupted to share a set of contradictory views on market conditions. Ryan noticed the investor frown. Then the investor countered the CEO with different data. The CEO in turn introduced more data supporting his own position.

Ryan had no idea what was going on at first. Back and forth the investor and CEO parried each other with knowledge of market conditions. The discussion seemed barely relevant. For ten minutes the skirmish continued. And for ten minutes the meeting went nowhere. Then it clicked – this discussion wasn't about business, it was about posturing. These guys were trying to one-up each other. Despite the cold outdoors, tempers indoors flared. The investor was becoming visibly angry. The meeting did not look good. If something didn't change soon, the deal was going to collapse.

Most of us have witnessed posturing take place. We are told power in groups comes from posturing. But what exactly is being postured? Do we puff out our chests? Should we act pompous and talk down to everyone? The last chapter showed us that personal power is rooted in a feeling of control, an internal orientation, and a focus on action. But how does personal power translate into real power in groups?

To understand power in groups, first we need to look at group psychology. Hierarchy is how groups organize based on status. But formal hierarchies outlined in management books won't help us. Intellectual idealisms are often disconnected from the real world. We must explore the roots of hierarchy absent of institutional influence. To do this, let's step out of the skyscrapers and turn to life on the streets.

Down and Dirty

The late 1800s were a rough time for Southern Italians. Disease and natural disasters wracked the land. Malaria was on the rise. The great Mount Vesuvius that once buried the Roman city of Pompeii erupted again. At the same time, the government in the north imposed harsh taxes on southern farmers and fisherman. These taxes squeezed workers. As challenge and starvation mounted, Italians cast their gaze across the Atlantic to the land of opportunity, America.[1]

Italian immigration to the U.S. peaked at the turn of the 20th century. Immigration was driven almost entirely by southerners from Mezzogiorno. Tens of thousands of Southern Italians flooded into Boston. The majority of Italians settled in Boston's North End, which offered inexpensive housing and easy access to jobs throughout the city. The neighborhood soon became known as Little Italy. But despite the promise of opportunity, immigrants faced new challenges. Crowded tenement houses lined the streets. The lack of English-speaking skills led to discrimination. The lack of money led to exploitation. Many Italians found themselves caught up in the Padrone System, an arrangement that forced workers into slave-like relationships with job contractors. The Italian slum arose. The slum had no institutional authority. Those in the slum lived by the law of the jungle.

The Nortons were a tough gang of Italian teens that prowled the North End slum.[2] These boys lacked formal education but instinctively knew how to stay alive in the urban jungle. Every boy found his way into a gang, and every gang had their turf. The Nortons centered their turf at a corner on Norton Street.

When Doc found his way into the Nortons, he was a scrappy kid who'd already been in several fights. Despite his modest physical stature, he had charisma and a quick wit. The leader of the Nortons respected Doc but enjoyed roughing him up. These rough-ups weren't public and Doc tolerated the pain. One afternoon the leader picked a fight with Doc in front of the entire gang. Doc knew that getting pounded in public would affect how the other boys saw him. With his reputation on the line, Doc retaliated. After a short scuffle, Doc pinned the leader to the ground and demanded they stop fighting. The leader agreed. But when Doc let him up, the leader smacked Doc in the face.

Blood poured out of Doc's nose, sending Doc into a frenzy. Doc battered the leader back down and punched him repeatedly until the gang broke them apart. After that, Doc ran the gang and the other boys listened to him.

This is the law of the jungle, and what we expect in a gang hierarchy. The strongest dominates by crushing dissenters. *Lord of the Flies* epitomized this jungle-like nature of humans.[3] The fictional story tells of a group of boys marooned on a deserted island in the Pacific Ocean. The boys' attempt at self-governing quickly dissolve into chaos and savagery as they vie for power. When the boys are eventually rescued, three of them lie dead from the internal strife. The story illustrates the law of the jungle in action.

But what if we have the law of the jungle all wrong?

One evening in 1965, six teenage boys from Tonga set off on a fishing trip with only a few sacks of bananas and coconuts.[4] Hours later they were caught in a storm. Their sail and rudder broke, leaving them adrift for days. Eventually they washed ashore on the deserted island of Ata. Here they would spend the next year alone before being rescued. It was a real-life *Lord of the Flies* story.

So what happened on that island?

The group set up a small garden for food, mechanisms to collect rainwater, and a permanent fire. They survived on fish, fruit, and wild animals. And they made a pact to never quarrel. When quarrels inevitably broke out, the boys instituted self-imposed time-outs. Everything was shared and every thing was focused on survival. When the boys were finally rescued, not only were they all in excellent health, but the bonds they forged together on that island lasted the rest of their lives.

We can't understand power in groups if we don't understand the evolutionary purpose of hierarchy. Hierarchy is how groups organize to flourish. Our position in a hierarchy represents the value we bring to a group.[5] Value is the crux. In other words, our position in a hierarchy is an acknowledgement of our contribution to the group's identity and goals. Group psychology doesn't foster conflict, it fosters survival. That is why the real story of the Tongan boys is completely different than the fictional *Lord of the Flies*.*

In the real jungle among hunter–gatherer tribes, the best hunters were awarded the most status because they were crucial to group survival.[6] Status had nothing to do with physical dominance per se. Research suggests groups often punish those who try to take power by force. It was simply taken for granted that the person who brought the most value to the group was considered the most important in the group.

Doc's rise to power in the Nortons wasn't about group dominance, it was about group survival. Territorial scuffles broke out frequently between rival gangs in the slum. Toughness was the crux of group survival because the Nortons had to defend themselves. If someone from another gang beat up a Norton, the leader had to go and beat up the aggressor. Toughness was the currency of value not because it was used to dominate group members,

---

*Muzafer Sherif ran a series of intergroup conflict experiments in the 1950s to create a situation similar to that in *Lord of the Flies*. During summer camp, Muzafer split boys into two teams competing against one another for prizes. His first experiment at Camp Middle Grove completely failed.[22] Boys remained friends despite being split up into competing teams. Muzafer even tried to incite conflict by pretending to be one team while stealing clothes and sabotaging equipment of the other team. No luck. The following year, Muzafer ran his second and now famous Robber Cave Experiment.[23] By carefully keeping the teams separated and ignorant of each other the first few days of summer camp, and then intentionally setting the teams up for competition after they met, Muzafer successfully manipulated the teams to be enemies. But it took a lot of work to set up conflict reminiscent of *Lord of the Flies*. The conflict was virtually eliminated when the teams had to work together later to secure drinking water, a basic resource. Survival doesn't split us apart, it brings us together.

but because it was used to support them.* Doc demonstrated his strength when he overpowered the original leader. After that, Doc used his strength to protect the group. The Nortons quickly learned to trust Doc. Even the ousted leader would become a close confidant.

In the 2000 Presidential Election, George. W. Bush and Al Gore faced off in three Town Hall debates. Audiences felt Gore was too soft in the first two debates. The President is obviously one of the most powerful positions in the world. Nobody wants a weak leader. When the third debate rolled around at a town-hall style setup in St. Louis, Gore sought to show strength. Early in the debate, Gore used his physical presence in a jungle-like bid to intimidate Bush. As Bush responded to a question, Gore squared his shoulders and strode up to within a couple feet of Bush to literally hover over him.[7] Did Gore's gambit work?

Bush glanced at Gore. It was an awkward moment for everyone. And then Bush showed . . . no reaction. Bush paused for a second, gave an amused nod to his opponent, and went back to answering the question. Gore was left standing there with a grimace on his face. Gore's graceless attempt at dominance completely backfired. Those watching took note. As one viewer commented, it was a collision between an acting alpha and a real alpha.[8] Bush came off powerful in a moment that mattered. When the average age of incoming Presidents is 55, clearly physical strength is not the core value required for the position.

The Nortons disbanded their gang when they reached adulthood. Doc stayed in Boston's North End while the other members left the city. A decade later circumstances brought the gang back together. Doc had built a large local network

---

*Dominance is covered in Chapter 8. We cannot fully understand dominance until we understand personal power. Dominance is actively disempowering others. Fostering personal power is one pathway to alleviate countless issues in society related to dominance such as exclusion.

during the interim. When gang members needed work, Doc used his connections to provide support. Doc also organized social events with other groups. Although Doc had a withered arm and was now far from strongest, the group entrusted him once again with leadership. Why? Because Doc now served the group's mature needs. Not once did Doc or anyone under him exert authority through physical force as adults. The currency of group value had changed.

Doc's story gives us a glimpse into life on the streets. Doc was raised in the slum unprotected by the authority of institutions. Our myth is that the jungle, real or urban, is a dog-eat-dog world. But people are not inherently monsters, they're survivors. We survive by serving those who serve us. Doc understood that his status in a world without laws required delivering value to others. We can take these basic lessons from a world without rules and bring them into our world.

Moving Up

Rice University is known as the "Harvard of the South." Located in Houston, Texas, it ranks as one of the top universities in the United States. Past presidents of Rice include world experts in science, founders of international organizations, and fantastic fundraisers. Rice is known foremost for its Engineering School, which invests upwards of $80 million in research each year.

When Reginald "Reggie" DesRoches was invited to be the dean of Rice Engineering, he gladly accepted. Reggie is a Haitian immigrant with buoyant energy and a sideways smile. Becoming dean of Rice Engineering was a big step up for Reggie, but he was prepared after having served as chair of the top ranked Civil Engineering Program at Georgia Tech. Reggie could have comfortably remained dean at Rice until the day he retired. But that's not what happened.

Five years after Reggie moved to Rice, he became the president of Rice University.

To give you an idea of what this means, in five years Reggie went from the equivalent of a mid-level manager to CEO. Now he regularly meets with global academic and political leaders. Reggie is the epitome of success. I had to know how he did it, so I called him up.

As dean, Reggie told me one of his first goals was to construct a new building on campus. A new building would make space for more research. But deans for the last thirty years had tried and failed to construct a new building. Previous deans explained how a new building would benefit the Engineering School. But the construction cost was roughly $150 million. There was no money and less interest. The goal remained a pipe dream.

Reggie established relationships with potential stakeholders. He met 300 alumni his first year at Rice. During a trip to California, Reggie's typical day included morning coffee with one alum, lunch with another, topped off by dinner with a third. On repeat. He got to know each alum's background and ambitions. Then Reggie put forth his building proposal to the Rice Board of Trustees. The Board was composed of Rice alumni, many of whom he already met. And this was where Reggie differed from his predecessors. Reggie explained how a new building would further the Trustees' ambitions, not just Engineering. Reggie provided data on Rice's mission and admissions, and he outlined exactly how the Trustees' goals would be achieved.

The Trustees green-lighted the proposal.

Reggie set to work raising money for the project through his new alumni network. And within three years, Reggie became university provost. He took charge of all academics across the university.

As provost, Reggie immediately hired an outside firm to collect data on Rice's research activities. He wanted to analyze how Rice could become even more competitive as an academic institution. Reggie shared the firm's insights with the Trustees. His actions showed a new precedent that spoke of *we can do better by moving forward* rather than resting on the laurels of the past. He established the Diversity, Equity, and Inclusion Office. He established several new majors. And in a nutshell, two years after transitioning into the role of Provost, Reggie was named Rice University's new president.

One could write a book on Reggie's leadership skills that landed him the top job. In fact, you're essentially holding this book. But underneath all his skills rests one solid factor – Reggie knows how to add value to the people in the organization.

There are two types of value we bring to our work, maintaining value and creating value. Maintaining value means we meet the requirements of our role. Countless deans before Reggie did superb jobs. Many of them were equally qualified to take on more responsibility. So what allowed Reggie to achieve greater success?

Climbing the hierarchy is built on adding value to the group, not asking the group for help. High-power people come in with solutions, not problems. Senior managers are looking for staff to help them achieve their goals, they are not there to help you achieve yours. Whereas prior engineering deans asked for support to construct a new building on campus, Reggie explained how a new building would benefit the Trustees whose support he needed. Reggie framed his actions as delivering value to his superiors. This made Reggie both valuable and persuasive. This also makes him one of the most successful people I have ever met. Now let's take a closer look at what it means to be persuasive.

Speak Value

Andrew is a millionaire whom I helped pitch his first startup to exit. He is one of the most down-to-Earth founders I know. He grew up on a small farm in Spain and carried his rural values of hard work and care to the big city. After selling his company,

Andrew tinkered with new business ideas. He developed a tracking system to help retailers monitor product distribution. One of his first customers was a major beverage company operating on four continents. The company also struggled to track the billions of products they shipped globally each year.

Andrew drove to the customer's office to meet with a VP named Birk. The two men shook hands. Usually at the start of a meeting, salespeople engage in casual chitchat before diving into a discussion of the product. That's not Andrew's style. After shaking hands, Andrew sidestepped the usual chitchat and went straight to the point. Birk wanted to expand his influence inside the beverage company. To grow, Birk needed to cut costs. Andrew explained that tracking products would provide insight into cost-cutting. "You're a cash cow for these big consulting companies," Andrew said. "But we can learn and grow together, not like the usual supplier–customer relationship. We'll help you grow if you help us grow." That was Friday. The following Monday they had a commitment in place.

Persuasion is the language of influence. You can't be powerful if you can't persuade others to support you. Andrew understood the real value in the transaction wasn't supporting the beverage company, it was supporting Birk's career. Birk was the decision-maker, so Andrew went straight to the value for Birk. This is Andrew's secret to starting two successful companies. It also shows us the root of persuasion.

Persuasion positions value, not ideas.[9] When startup founders enlist me to enhance their pitches, I share with them the most basic rule of success. *Bad pitches focus on the product, good pitches focus on the value of the product.* No one purchases a product for the sake of the product, they invest in the value the product delivers. We don't buy a toothbrush to own a plastic stick with bristles, we buy it to have clean teeth.

Jay Conger spent a decade observing the keys to persuading senior business leaders.[10] It's important to persuade senior leadership in order to secure resources for new projects. Jay found that one of the most important keys to persuasion at executive levels is to "frame for common ground." Jay noted that you need to explain how your idea will benefit the person you're trying to gain support from. Whether you're trying to win support from an executive, a colleague, or a client, explain how your ideas will achieve their goals.

Value is in the eye of the beholder. Every person has a different priority. As I wrote in my book *Magnetic*, one of my close friends was a top salesperson at Oracle. She regularly met with new customers to sell them Oracle software. When she met with a customer's CFO, she shared how Oracle would save the company money. When she met with their CEO, she shared how Oracle would further the corporate vision. And when she met with an engineer, she explained how Oracle training would look good on their resume when they changed jobs. Her sales pitch was always about what was in it for the person sitting in front of her.

Because value is in the eye of the beholder, the value is not in your ideas. It's not in what you do, it's in how others perceive what you do. That is why communicating your value is essential to securing external power. Most of the time when we speak, we're so caught up explaining the facts and features of our ideas that we forget to explain why those facts and features are important to the people in front of us. Not to the world, not necessarily to the organization, but to the goals of the people we're talking to. How you speak about your work is how others perceive the value of your work. For example, do you focus on detailing your product features, or do you focus on solving the customer's problems and providing them benefits?

Andrew closed the deal with Birk because he understood it was Birk, not a faceless amorphous beverage organization, he had to win over. Birk cared about cost-cutting. Although tracking products has nothing to do with cost-cutting on the surface, Andrew secured Birk's business because he explained how tracking products fulfilled Birk's cost-cutting needs.

The focus on value is why we respect competence. Competence conveys your ability to deliver results, and it shows up in language when you reference your skills, knowledge, and reputation on the current topic. When people with high personal power persuade others, they instinctively focus on communicating signs of competence.[11,*] And the more someone communicates competence, the more they are valued by the group.[12] Thus, personal power translates naturally into social status.

Speak Action

Let's shift gears and test whether you can spot personal power through just a few written sentences. Read the following vignettes below by two people discussing taking a job overseas. Which feels more powerful to you?

1. *I'm not sure about going. On one hand, it seems like a good opportunity to learn a different culture and change paths in life. On the other hand, I am not sure that I want to accept everything that comes with it.*
2. *I made the decision to go and immerse myself in the culture. Now, I need to plan everything to prepare to go. First, I need to go online and find a plane ticket. Then, I will have to apply for a passport and visa.*

Over 100 Stanford students were presented with small vignettes like these and asked to rate how powerful the writers were.[13] Students rated the person who wrote the second

---

*Personal agency focuses on goals, which in turn focuses attention on information relevant to the achievement of goals (i.e., skills and abilities).

vignette as significantly more powerful than the first one. I'm guessing you did too.*

But why is the second one more powerful?

The first example shows someone deliberating about taking a job. The second example shows someone implementing their decision. Implementation conveys a focus on action, and action is power.**

The research also showed that U.S. Presidents who speak powerfully focus on implementing action. Throughout George W. Bush's 2000 Presidential campaign, he made strong promises to the American people. He repeated those promises in his victory acceptance speech:

Together, we will work to make all our public schools excellent, teaching every student of every background and every accent, so that no child is left behind. Together we will save Social Security and renew its promise of a secure retirement for generations to come. Together we will strengthen Medicare and offer prescription drug coverage to all of our seniors.[14]

Imagine if Bush had delivered a more deliberative message, "Together we will analyze the quality of education in our country. We will also explore whether Medicare is working or not." Doesn't sound nearly as powerful, does it? Bush might not have been elected President had his promises been deliberative. Unfortunately, we read weak headlines from both corporate and political leaders all the time. For example, "So-and-so CEO considering how to handle the new crisis,"

---

*This goes almost without saying now, but for those who still believe body language and tone of voice are the main vehicles of power, notice that even in the absence of body language and tone of voice, most people easily identify someone's power though their words.

**Both vignettes were rated equally competent and knowledgeable, meaning that power is more than a function of competence.

or "So-and-so leader debating how to respond to an international event."

Actions speak loud in our words. A focus on action is the delivery vehicle of value. When you want to be seen as powerful, come in with a plan.

But what if you don't have a plan? In these cases, elicit thoughts from your team. After all, the purpose of meetings is often to share knowledge and create a plan. Let others deliberate and you facilitate the deliberation. When everyone has spoken, you are now in a position to synthesize what you heard into a plan of action. You will appear more powerful by offering solutions and implementation plans than by spending your energy on deliberation. And setting implementation plans creates a readiness to act, pushing you more into your personal power.[15]

Give and Be Seen

Professor Corinne Bendersky wanted to understand how MBA students rise and fall in group hierarchies at UCLA.[16] MBA groups provide a perfect backdrop for real business because these students are both very smart and very competitive. When the academic year started, Corinne organized her students into teams to work on assignments together for the term. She measured the status of each student shortly after the teams formed, and then again at the end of the course ten weeks later. Status represents one's informal position in a hierarchy.

Corinne's results showed that regardless of a student's initial status, their position in the team hierarchy could change over time. But more importantly, she identified the behaviors that led to those shifts.

Students who gained status were the most generous with their teammates. It was that simple. Specifically, generous students gave helpful and constructive feedback. They were flexible and tried to accommodate others' needs. As a result, they were sought out more frequently for answers (which provided them more opportunity to deliver value). Conversely, those who were least generous, even if they started at the top, lost status over time. As we give, we go up.

A similar set of experiments was run in England in which students were grouped together and each student received a fixed amount of money.[17] Students could keep the money for themselves or donate some of it to a group fund. Money donated to the group fund was multiplied by two and redistributed across the group. In this way, donating to the group created more money for everyone overall but less for the giver. The results showed that those who donated the most to the fund earned more respect and were more likely to be chosen as group leaders. Generosity pays.

Generosity isn't merely connected to external power. Research in neuroscience revealed that when people donate money to charities supporting causes they care about, the Behavioral Approach System lights up.[*,18] The same area in the brain linked to personal power is linked to generosity. When our values align with the group, it is both inwardly and outwardly powerful to give.

Another demonstration of generosity is our commitment to the cause. In my twenties I worked at a semiconductor company in Japan. I was impressed with the Japanese level of commitment. They came to the office early and left only after the boss left. I would literally stay in the office until 11pm with the team waiting for the boss to go home. Then I'd drag my feet in the next morning at 9am, only to be the last one to arrive. Strong commitment was also true of Bob Iger, the CEO of Disney. Early in his career at ABC, Bob was one of the first to arrive in

---

*Specifically, the mesolimbic area associated with reward.

the office in the wee hours of the morning. Bob's early arrival showed his commitment to the company and contributed to his rapid rise up the ranks.[19]

Thus power comes from both capability and contribution. At a basic psychology level, we humans are quite like chimpanzees. In the wild, male chimpanzees who successfully attract mates are those who are the most capable of gathering food and the most likely to share the food they gather.[20] Obviously when a male chimp can't gather food, they are ignored regardless of how generous they are. Years ago when I worked at Merrill Lynch in Tokyo, one of my colleagues arrived before most everyone else and left late into the night. His commitment was clear. But despite these long hours, he didn't produce results. A VP on the floor confided to me that he wasn't sure my colleague would make it. A year after I left, I emailed my colleague at his Merrill Lynch address only to have it bounce. Even with commitment, delivering value is critical. However, when chimpanzees gather a lot of food and don't share it, they are also ignored.

Generosity does have a cost. In the MBA research at UCLA, the most generous team members received worse final grades in the course because the time they spent helping their team took away from the time they spent on individual course assignments. Likewise, group members in England who donated money to the group fund ended up with less money for themselves. And in Japan, workers were exhausted arriving early and staying late. But the silver lining is that the more the cost to give increases, the more status is earned by the giving.

In all the cases above, one additional factor was crucial – visibility. Generosity only mattered when others saw it. For example, when students in England donated money to the group fund but all donations were anonymous, those who donated more did not gain more status. Disney CEO Bob Iger came to work early when he was a junior employee, but what made his commitment noticeable was the fact that the business owners also came in early and spoke with him every morning.

Your generosity must be visible to the group for the group to recognize you. This is why socially connected people in the office often get promoted more rapidly.[21] Social connections provide more visibility to display generosity and commitment. Many people disempower themselves by blaming office politics as the cause for their lack of growth. But what people confuse as distasteful politics is often just visibility. If you keep your head down and nose to the grindstone, and that's all you do, no one will see you. When you are not seen, you are not valued. People cannot evaluate what they cannot see. That is why the best way to play politics in the office is to visibly add value to the influential people in your hierarchy.* Adding visible value is human psychology, there is nothing unnatural about it. In fact, it's the most natural thing in the world.

Value Over Posture

At the start of the chapter, when Ryan and his colleagues met with their main investor to close a $12 million deal for their aviation startup, the meeting devolved into posturing. Both the investor and Ryan's CEO got stuck in trying to one-up each other. As their voices grew louder, they created a cacophony of echoes off the white marble walls. Several minutes passed as the deal looked like it might go south. Ryan watched from the sidelines feeling at first confused, then impatient. He knew if he didn't step in soon, the meeting would collapse.

Ryan finally interrupted the discussion. He didn't understand posturing, but as COO he understood the nuts and bolts

---

*It is also important to know the process by which your company promotes employees. Sometimes what we mistake for politics is a misunderstanding of the process by which our value is evaluated.

of the company. He shared a few facts about operations to redirect the conversation. Both the investor and CEO turned their attention to Ryan. Ryan expanded on how operations affected their market position. Then he proposed actions the company could take to strengthen their position. The tone of the meeting shifted. The CEO listened. The investor leaned in and began asking questions about various performance indicators. Ryan continued to focus on the bottom-line and propose pathways in which the company could grow. An hour later when the meeting concluded, Ryan commanded the respect of everyone in that room. This wasn't a final decision-making moment, but it was a big step forward to secure the remaining investment.

Ultimately the company received the money. Along the way the CEO made several other mistakes and got ousted. The board invited Ryan to become CEO, but Ryan turned down the offer to take a motorcycle trip across South America. He preferred leather jackets to lavish suits. Eventually everybody won because the company was sold in a flush acquisition deal.

Evolutionary psychology focuses on group success. Regardless of where you stand in your group hierarchy today, give to others to go up. Seek ways to communicate and visibly add value to the group and its members. Communicating and delivering value is the fundamental pathway to personal power and status in groups. It is also only the first step. Communicating value prepares you to implement the next step. The next step is a much stronger display of your personal power and one of the greatest strengths of leaders.

The Power of Mental Preparation

We add value when we are goal-focused. One simple way researchers found to tap into your personal power and enhance your goal focus is to recall a time in the past you had power.

When you reflect on a previous time you had power, you activate a constellation of thoughts and feelings that trigger your feelings of power again in the moment. As a result, you will find it easier to add value.

To practice this exercise, recall a time when you had power over another person or a group of people. You may have controlled the ability of people to get what they wanted, or you might have been evaluating others. Write about the situation, what happened, how you felt, and any other details that brings the situation to mind. Spend a few minutes and at least half a page writing.[24]

You can use this exercise for any situation you want to walk in feeling powerful. For example, researchers found that when you practice this recall exercise before an interview, you significantly increase the odds of getting the job.[25]

Be sure you go through the practice completely each time you use it. Through the process of recall and writing, you activate the network of neurons in your mind associated with your personal power. The exercise is an emotional power pose. Like warming up the body, the process of recalling and writing warms up the power circuits of the mind so they're humming when you need them.

4 | Zoom Out

Rick Warren is the man you want in your corner. He's a jolly fellow who counsels people going through tough times. Rick stays at people's bedsides when they're sick and he attends funerals when their loved ones pass away. His energy feels like that of a beloved uncle you see on the holidays. His matter-of-fact voice is full of warmth. You wouldn't guess on first glance that Rick commands considerable power.

Rick is a pastor in California. He established his church in Saddleback Valley at the young age of 27. Rick grew his congregation into the tens of thousands through the following decades. His message of purpose was so popular that his first book, *The Purpose-Driven Life*, shipped over 25 million copies. It was a mega best-seller. Both Christians and non-Christians flocked to Rick's words. Members of President George W. Bush's administration were seen reading his book. During the 2008 Presidential Election, candidates John McCain and Barack Obama held a forum at Rick's church. Rick would subsequently deliver the invocation at President Obama's inauguration. The list goes on. Rick followed a singular purpose to build a church that carries the message of God.

Then Rick's son committed suicide.

Rick was powerful. But a day later he was destroyed. How does someone with personal power handle tragedy? Rick stopped conducting sermons, stopped meeting others, and isolated himself at home.[1]

Most books on personal growth advertise a common list of benefits – be happier, healthier, and more resilient. Power includes these benefits. The greater your personal power, the more resilient you become.[2] Part of what contributes to this resilience is that powerful people see the world differently. This perspective is what separates the shepherd from the flock.

Did Rick see the world differently, and where was his resilience?

Flying High

The 1960s are associated with a liberal spring of free love. People sought new experiences. They got high. They spaced out. Perhaps it's no surprise that the 1960s were the most defining years for space travel. The Cold War was in full effect. Russia and the U.S. competed at everything from military might to engineering achievement. In April of 1961, Russian cosmonaut Yuri Gagarin became the first man in space. It was a brilliant leap for humankind overshadowed only by the huge blow it dealt to America's public image. The news of Yuri spurred President John F. Kennedy to action. A month later on May 25, JFK delivered one of the most arousing messages of the 20th century – "I believe that this nation should commit itself to achieving the goal, before this decade is out, of landing a man on the moon and returning him safely to the Earth."[3] His words cemented a vision in the minds of millions. Everyone is familiar with Neil Armstrong and Buzz Aldrin's subsequent moon landing. But more remarkable still is that most everyone is equally familiar with JFK's words on that May day in 1961. The question is, what makes JFK's message of sending a man to the moon as enduring as the moon landing itself? The answer is that the message was concrete.

Concrete language is specific and tangible, focusing on details that often relate to our senses – things we can visualize for example, like an apple or a bouquet of roses. It is precisely because we can visualize JFK's words of a man on the moon that we remember it. We see it in our mind's eye. The opposite of concrete is abstract. Abstract language connects ideas and takes a broader perspective. The abstract thinker might see an apple and call it nutrition or describe a bouquet of roses as a sign of someone's love. Compared to abstract language, concrete descriptions of objects and events are more memorable.[4] In addition, customers who are marketed merchandise concretely are more satisfied.[5]

With this in mind, let's take a quick test to assess your personal power right now. Give yourself a few seconds to read the following question and choose either A or B.

Which of the following best describes voting for you?
A. *Marking a ballot*
B. *Influencing the election*

You might describe voting as marking a ballot. Or you might say that voting influences the election. The first is concrete, the second is abstract.

Pamela Smith explored how powerful people process information by asking them to describe voting just as you did.[6] Her research uncovered one of the most important discoveries of power to date – *personal power makes us think and speak more abstractly* (they chose B).

In a follow-up experiment, Pamela found that when people spoke in more abstract language, they were seen as a better fit for management. Pamela and her colleagues also showed that politicians were seen as more powerful when describing current events in abstract terms versus concrete terms.[7] When President Obama delivered his victory speech upon winning the Presidential election in 2008, he began with the abstract words,

"If there is anyone out there who still doubts that America is a place where all things are possible; who still wonders if the dream of our founders is alive in our time; who still questions the power of our democracy, tonight is your answer."[8] Concrete messages may be more memorable, but they don't convey more power.* We'll get back to JFK's words shortly.

The Big Picture

Mark designs missiles, the kind that defend nations. Militaries of major governments depend on Mark to outfit their navies. Mark is one of the top minds at a major defense company that develops these missiles, satellites, and other defense equipment. By all appearances, Mark is very much the stereotypical engineer. Dressing up for him means business casual. He's just as happy solving world-class technical problems as he is playing Wordle. But he thinks different.

To give you an example of how Mark thinks, he took on the project to develop a new missile for the United States Navy. His team needed a more effective epoxy (glue) to seal the components together. Mark tasked a senior manager to identify the best epoxy. The manager in turn tasked a junior engineer to bring back a list of options. A week later the team reconvened. Mark opened the meeting with an agenda, led through several items on the list, and eventually came to the epoxy. The junior engineer stood up and flashed a spreadsheet on the screen showing

---

*Communicating power also plays out visually in pictures and text. Pictures are concrete, whereas text is abstract. The use of emojis (pictures) to replace words in text messages was rated as less powerful than strictly using words.[33] Texters who used words over emojis were seen as more suitable for management. Similarly, when wearing a sports jersey containing either a team logo or the name of the team, fans displaying a team name on their jersey were seen as more powerful than those displaying a logo. However, it's important to note that pictures reduce social distance whereas words, while more powerful, create more social distance. Around friends and family, you may want to choose closeness.

his data. "This epoxy is the strongest and therefore the best," said Junior, confidently pointing to the top of the list.

By all accounts, Junior was correct. As every good employee knows, the quality of a product is only as good as the quality of the material.

Mark cleared his throat vocally, and all eyes turned to him. In these situations, Mark has one question he asks junior employees. According to Mark, this one question provides him 100% accuracy in determining whether the junior employee is ready for a promotion or not.

"What's the cost of this epoxy?" Mark asked.

Junior glanced at the spreadsheet. Then Junior fumbled through a few papers and shrugged. Junior had no idea. Mark shook his head. In Mark's view, Junior was a million miles away from being promoted. Junior had no perspective.

Defense companies are businesses. If these companies can't develop products that are both high performance and cost effective, customers won't buy. Mark's role is to maintain a clear view of the project goals and the various factors required to achieve those goals. One of the most important factors is cost. Junior's exclusive focus on performance showed that he had tunnel vision. There's nothing wrong with tunnel vision when it's needed to solve a dense problem. But tunnel vision alone is not high-power management material. Value is measured by contribution to the larger goals of the group, not the smaller transactions. Powerful people focus on the big picture.

The higher you are in the hierarchy, the greater your perspective must be. In manufacturing, the floor worker knows exactly how many bolts are required to attach one piece of metal to the next. The manager looks to improve efficiencies in the assembly line. The executive evaluates corporate strategy. Each perspective widens to include those below it. As the perspective widens, the perspective becomes more abstract. This is why leaders often get the gist of things even when they don't know all the details. Powerful people see the forest from the trees.

I coached a product manager at Google. She came to me because she was interested in strengthening her status in the company. Before we met, she focused exclusively on communicating her technical expertise, the trees. Our first meeting reoriented her to communicate value. As my client explored ways to convey her value to management, she sought to understand what management valued.* She began seeing the division's larger goals, the forest. As her perspective widened, her ability to communicate her value expanded. Her relationship with management grew in equal proportion. To appear powerful, you must focus on the forest even when you're working with the trees.

Focusing on the big picture also changes the nature of conversations. Most of us habitually focus on winning an argument. Conversely a powerful person can look to the larger goal of the interaction rather than the content of what's being discussed. Instead of arguing who is right, the powerful person can analyze the outcome they desire and engage in ways that will achieve the desired outcome. Healthy couples do this frequently, focusing on the relationship and not just the topic being discussed. Parents are also familiar with this thinking. When a child is having a meltdown, effective parents manage the child and not the argument.

Share Your View

If the big picture is a sign of power, then it follows that those who aren't fully in their power don't always see it. Tim was one of those employees who needed perspective. Tim's normally soft features were hard as ice the day he received his performance review. He stormed down the hall, daggers lancing from his eyes. Colleagues scurried out of his way. Tim had been assigned to lead a new multi-million-dollar project for one of his company's top clients. He worked around the clock.

---

*Because leaders often see the big picture, the leader's needs serve as a proxy for the group's needs. To rise up the career ladder, focus on meeting the needs of those above you.

He achieved phenomenal results. But when his performance review came around, he was marked "average." He was furious. The low gray cubicle walls on both sides of the aisle passed by in a blur as he marched straight into his director's office. The director looked up and waved Tim to take a seat. Tim slammed the door behind him and exploded. He shared his contributions and results. His shock at being marked average. His feelings of betrayal. His voice boomed with anger. The office windows rattled. The director sat quietly and listened.

"What's your real problem Tim?" the director asked calmly.

And that was it. There was no defense, no justification. The director went straight to the heart of the matter. Tim's surprise completely deflated his anger.

After a few moments, Tim confided he was there to earn a living for his family. Tim received a promotion the year before. He took his effort up another notch to show outstanding performance and receive additional compensation.

The director nodded. He punched a few keys on his computer and flipped the monitor around so Tim could see. The screen displayed Tim's salary increase with the performance review. It was commensurate to outstanding performance. Tim would receive the financial compensation he desired. The director explained that he had to save the "outstanding" title for another employee he planned to promote. This was a matter of internal process. Tim relaxed. He was good with that.

The big picture allows leaders to separate the key issues from the noise. "We cannot solve our problems from the same [level of] thinking we used when we created them," said Einstein. We hear these words quoted all the time. Seeing the big picture is what these words mean. Getting to the heart of the matter isn't about zeroing in, it's about zooming out.

SpaceX literally built their business on affordable rocketry. Elon Musk hired former NASA engineers to build SpaceX's first rockets. Initially, most NASA engineers overlooked material costs during design. Like the junior engineer at the major defense company, NASA engineers didn't take the big picture of business into account. Unlike the junior engineer however, these NASA veterans were the crème de la crème of rocket scientists. It wasn't that the engineers lacked perspective. The engineers were operating in a new and unfamiliar environment. NASA's budget priorities are far different than those of a private company. The engineers needed a new perspective. Elon trained the team to take costs into account when selecting materials for the build.[9] After receiving guidance, the engineers quickly adjusted to their new environment. Today everyone is familiar with SpaceX thanks to the success of Elon and his team. And this is why leaders are placed on top. Their personal power provides them perspective, and they use this perspective to guide others. Perspective is one of the myriad ways in which internal personal power equips one to secure external formal power.

When you find yourself in a meeting and stuck in the weeds, one of the simplest acts of power you can take is to step back and say, "what's the bigger goal here?" In doing so, you widen the perspective of the group and reorient awareness toward priorities. People will notice how you think.

Every great leader and change-maker communicated from a fundamentally different perspective of the world. This is why truly brilliant minds appear both unique and effortless. They anchor themselves in the higher abstract view. Their social power comes from communicating their unique perspective to those around them. When powerful people speak, they translate their perspective to the level of their audience. They can move smoothly between the forest and the trees, making connections no one else sees. For the speaker these connections are obvious, but to listeners they sound extraordinary. This perspective is why we turn to leaders to guide us.

Let's circle back to pastor Rick Warren. There are no words to describe the feelings Rick must have experienced when his son committed suicide. As Rick explains it, he spent months in isolation with his wife and God. His wife Kay was equally consumed with loss. Kay had written a book years before called, *Choose Joy*. She wore a necklace with those two words inscribed. Rick kept asking, "how do you choose joy when your heart is breaking in a million pieces?"[10] But there was a bigger picture to be seen, and they sought it. Slowly they began to make sense of their pain and see beyond this one tragic event. Before the death of his son, Rick served those who suffered with poverty and AIDS. He donated most of his income to people in need. He hosted the 2006 Global Summit on AIDS. Now Rick realized he could expand his work to serve people struggling with mental illness. It wasn't what he asked for and it wasn't what he planned, but it was the path he saw laid out for him.*

---

*Surrender is a concept frequently associated with faith, and appears to be the antithesis of a feeling of control. Yet the power of surrender is found in many spiritual and recovery traditions. In recovery, steps two and three in The Twelve Steps of Alcoholics Anonymous (AA) are, "Came to believe that a Power greater than ourselves could restore us to sanity," and "Made a decision to turn our will and our lives over to the care of God as we understood Him."[34] What is often being surrendered in AA is the compulsion for the addiction or the compulsion for control, which are reactive ways of being.[35] Those who surrender sometimes view the act of surrender as choosing to take a courageous leap of faith.[36] Thus, choosing to surrender is an active choice, not a passive one. Research into AA suggests participants feel more empowered and responsible for their lives as a result of the program.

The act of surrender also repeatedly leads to well-being. A study of surrender among women with breast cancer showed that women who surrendered felt more peaceful, happy, and connected with something greater than the self.[37] This last part, something greater than the self, is most interesting. When we connect with something greater than ourselves, such as God, we connect to a much wider and abstract view of the world than the concrete situation facing us. We take on the big picture.

Equally interesting is that overall Locus of Control is not associated with surrender, meaning surrender relates to neither an internal nor external Locus.[38] Rather, internal Locus of Control is associated with a more benevolent and forgiving view of a higher power, and external Locus of Control is associated with a more negative and vindictive view of a higher power. Therefore, surrender both contributes to and is facilitated by personal power. When people surrender in the process of fostering personal power, surrender provides "the foundation for movement towards autonomy."[39]

"Your greatest ministry will come out of your deepest pain,"[11] Rick later confided. If you see Rick today, he wears a smile on his face with a buoyancy that belies tragedy. He inspires those suffering with mental illness to see the value of their lives and to understand their place in the universe. The positive message Rick shares with everyone is, "God made you to love you."[12]

You may admire Rick's leadership in hosting congregations of thousands. You may be inspired by his resilience. But Rick's power comes not from his popularity nor positivity. Rick's power comes from his ability to see the big picture. His perspective pulled him out of his darkness, and he uses his perspective to bring light to the lives of others.

Make New Meaning

In the early 1930s, thousands of banks shuttered their businesses. The financial collapse robbed Americans of their savings accounts. The loss of jobs and savings led to countless home foreclosures. With almost a quarter of the workforce unemployed, hunger plagued the United States. Hundreds of thousands of Americans were forced to set up homeless camps in parks. The narrative Americans had been fed about unfettered capitalism was killing the economy and stealing their lives. Helplessness and hopelessness reigned. The public was lost. All the while President Hoover failed to fix it.

Franklin D. Roosevelt entered the 1932 Presidential Election to run against Hoover.[13] FDR criticized Hoover's anti-regulatory stance that served corporate America at the expense of the American people. FDR crafted a new narrative to explain the cause of the current problems. He argued that the lack of government oversight had led to suffering, not growth. In a large banquet hall in San Francisco, FDR laid out a vision in which the government would intercede to resuscitate the economy.

He spoke of America as a nation of laborers. He spoke of universal principles. He ended with a plan of action to lead Americans out of their suffering with an economic declaration of rights, "Every man has a right to life; and this means that he has also a right to make a comfortable living."[14] Whereas Hoover represented the status quo, FDR represented change.

Hoover, by far the more experienced politician, defended against FDR's attacks by highlighting the gap in experience.[15] But it was for naught. FDR's New Deal captivated the minds of Americans. FDR's campaign slogan proclaimed, "happy days are here again." FDR won the election.

When I studied FDR's campaign, I couldn't help but notice the similarity with other Presidential campaigns this last century. It seems successful campaigns have a winning formula that shows up again and again. Can you spot it?

Fast forward to 1980. Stagflation became the status quo. The economy was paralyzed under the watch of President Jimmy Carter. The country was in the throes of confusion. Carter ran for reelection against the upstart Ronald Reagan that year.[16] Reagan came in with a new narrative that explained government regulation was the cause of suffering. Reagan offered a vision of deregulatory action that would "unleash [American citizens'] great strength and remove the roadblocks government has put in their way."[17] Whereas Carter represented the status quo, Reagan represented change.

President Carter, much like Hoover, attempted to run on experience. But it was for naught. Reagan's vision of deregulation captured the hearts and minds of Americans. Reagan's campaign slogan proclaimed, "we can make America great again."

You've heard Reagan's campaign slogan repeated in 2016. It's the President get-elected formula, and it's not new. Powerful people have a consistent way of speaking. This formula works on both sides of the political aisle. But what's fascinating is that the losers don't know it.

After the turn of the 21st century, the economy was again falling into financial crisis. During the 2008 Presidential Election, Barack Obama campaigned with a new narrative. Obama explained that unregulated Wall Street was the cause of the economic crisis. He offered new policies to support middle-class families and small businesses while clamping down on big bankers. Obama ran on the platform of change.[18]

Both Hillary Clinton in the primaries and John McCain in the election ran on platforms of experience, but it was for naught. Obama's vision won the hearts of Americans. His slogan, "Yes, we can."[19]

There is no secret to successful Presidential campaigns – candidates help voters make sense of their suffering by introducing a new big picture. This big picture reframes the cause of the problem. In this new frame of understanding, candidates offer a path of action that will solve the people's problems and lead them out of suffering.* And in every case, candidates offer hope. This is the secret to great leadership. This is the practice of being internally driven and action oriented. This is a demonstration of personal power being externally expressed.

Powerful people are meaning makers. They don't simply see the big picture, they create the big picture. They are the storytellers who make sense of a turbulent environment and use their story as a basis for action. Whether it is a U.S. President or a non-profit director, these leaders make meaning that provides the basis for groups to navigate the world. And followers expect leaders to take up this role, so it becomes an obligation of leadership.[20]

---

*Note how running on a platform of experience focuses on maintaining value while running on a platform of change focuses on creating value.

Light the Path

It's April 1961. Russia sends the first cosmonaut to space and returns him to Earth. Rather than celebrate this historic achievement, fear grips America. Headlines across the U.S. question whether Russia will plant its flag on the moon and on Mars. Will Communism dominate space? Space flight depends on rockets. The Germans used rockets as weapons of terror in World War II. Rockets carry atom bombs. Russian rocketry is now superior to the U.S. These are the thoughts going through the minds of the American people.[21]

JFK understands that he must take action to quell the fears racing through his country. JFK's focus is not on space, it's on survival. The people need hope and guidance. JFK gathers his advisors to create a plan. One month later, he unveils his vision:

> *If we are to win the battle that is now going on around the world between freedom and tyranny. . . . Now it is time to take longer strides, time for a great new American enterprise, time for this nation to take a clearly leading role in space achievement, which in many ways may hold the key to our future on Earth . . . But this is not merely a race. Space is open to us now, and our eagerness to share its meaning is not governed by the efforts of others. We go into space because whatever mankind must undertake, free men must fully share . . . I believe that this nation should commit itself to achieving the goal, before this decade is out, of landing a man on the moon and returning him safely to the Earth.*[22]

This was not a speech about sending a man to the moon, this was a speech about protecting the free world.

The ultimate big picture that channels energy toward action is the vision. Visions like JFK's speech are abstract objectives that focus on values and inform goals. People don't follow a leader per se, they follow the vision a leader represents. President Obama declared, "the way power works at every level, at the United

Nations or in your neighborhood, is, 'do you have a community that stands behind what you stand for?' And if you do, you'll have more power. And if you don't, you won't."[23]

Robert Baum conducted a study comparing performance of small businesses with and without a vision.[24] These owner-run operations had an average of 25 employees, making the CEOs effectively entrepreneurs. Among the 183 companies evaluated, Robert and his colleagues found that companies without a vision grew on average 5.5% year over year. Companies with a vision grew 12.4%. Visions correlated with more than double the growth rate, making them a critical component of leadership. Small businesses of 25 employees can be likened to the size of sports teams. You don't have to be the CEO of a large corporation to deliver a vision, you can deliver a vision to those around you today.

Robert's research also showed that successful visions had to be reiterated over and over again. Visions had to be shared in hallway conversations, meetings, and corporate events. Without consistent communication, visions did not impact revenue growth. When Steve Job spoke of visions during his time at NeXT Computer, he said:

> There needs to be someone who is the keeper and reiterator of the vision, because there's just a ton of work to do. And a lot of times when you have to walk a thousand miles and you take the first step, it looks like a long ways. And it really helps if there's someone there saying we're one step closer. The goal definitely exists, it's not just a mirage out there. So in a thousand and one little and sometimes larger ways the vision needs to be reiterated. I do that a lot.[25]

One of my favorite TED talks online is Simon Sinek's *How Great Leaders Inspire Action*. Simon proposed the golden circle to explain how effective leaders communicate. The golden circle is made up of three layers – WHY, HOW, and WHAT.[26] Most powerful is the WHY at the core of the circle, which anchors the group's values. The middle layer is the HOW, which communicates how to achieve those values. The outer layer is the WHAT, the products. It is a flow from the abstract to the concrete. JFK's moon speech fits firmly into this model, paraphrasing, 'we believe in freedom over tyranny. The way we promote freedom is to expand into space. We will do this by sending a man to the moon.'

What is your leadership style – do you exclusively focus the details/WHAT, can you communicate the approach/HOW, and are you able to frame the approach within a set of values/WHY? When you have a critical message to deliver, consider your level of abstraction. A wider perspective conveys your ability to meet the wider needs of the group. And your ability to meet those needs conveys your worthiness of a more privileged role within the group.

Visions are the natural language of those with personal power, and it is the nature of powerful people to be more effective leaders.

Bring Others into the Light

Keith owns a beach house in Florida that his family visits frequently. Living oceanside with children over the years made him conscious of rising sea levels from climate change. Most of us worry about climate change but feel powerless to fix it. Keith on the other hand was the VP of Strategic Planning at an international energy company. As the leader of corporate strategy, Keith turned his focus toward renewable energy. He wanted to speed up deployment of renewables across the world to combat climate change.

Keith set to work forecasting future energy demand for major nations. It was an enormous task broken down into many tiny pieces. Among those pieces was calculating solar and wind energy economics. Solar panels and wind turbines have fixed manufacturing costs, but they only provide intermittent power. When the sun goes down and the wind stops, the value of renewables lessens.

Keith called a midlevel engineer into his office. He tasked the engineer to analyze the value of these intermittent sources across the planet. It was a rather dull assignment on first blush, perhaps something even a junior engineer could do. Keith noticed a sour look flash briefly across the engineer's face. Accuracy was critical, and the last thing Keith needed was less-than-stellar precision due to a lack of motivation.

Keith kept the engineer in his office for a few extra minutes. Keith walked the engineer through how this seemingly mundane task was a crucial step to defining a much larger strategy. He explained that once the company knew the economics, they could use this data to predict and accelerate renewables deployment where it made the most sense. The result would impact the need for oil, gas, and nuclear energy across the planet. The task was vital to get right. After Keith finished speaking, the engineer left Keith's office walking a little straighter.

When Keith shared this story with me, he said that connecting the dots between small roles and big visions was so important in management that he made it a habit.

Great leaders connect the dots.* Every task no matter how small fits into the bigger picture, the vision. When you align others to a vision, you make it possible for them to align their values with the organization's values, triggering their Behavioral Approach System and empowering them. And when you connect other people's efforts to the vision, people start leaning into your leadership perspective.

---

*Check out Steve Jobs' commencement speech at Stanford.[40]

Carry the Torch Forward

Mike McCue is a self-made multi-millionaire. Raised on food stamps with a father who had terminal cancer, Mike learned at a young age that it was up to him to support his family. He founded and sold his first company for $20 million in his twenties.[27] He founded his second company in his thirties, a voice-recognition software for telephones called Tellme. Tellme was basically the 1999 version of Siri. The product allowed callers to voice commands over the phone that the system would recognize and respond to. Like all stereotypical Silicon Valley founders, Mike started Tellme out of his garage. Business boomed, and the garage got real small real fast. Mike raised $238 million from investors and hired hundreds of new employees. The influx required moving the office out of his garage and into a legitimate building. Mike organized the new office as a wide flat space without cubicles. In the middle of the open space was Mike's desk, surrounded like a donut by the employees of the company. Mike was both figuratively and literally at the center.

Mike elicited trust from his Tellme team through his crazy work-all-day and work-all-night attitude. Employees witnessed his commitment and energy, but more importantly they believed in his vision. He led with optimism and spoke positively of everyone and everything. It energized those around him. Many on his team were willing to march over hot coals for him.

Then the dot-com bubble burst. The market tanked.

Overnight the business landscape shifted. Mike saw death on the horizon for Tellme.[28] The next day he entered the office. He walked to his seat at the center. Then he slumped down and dropped his head to his desk. Mike felt immense pressure to keep the company going. He wanted to save jobs and pay back investors, but the challenge seemed insurmountable. Despair emanated

off him. It was the first time employees had ever witnessed this
behavior. This was not typical Mike. The room was completely
silent. Everyone in the office stared.

A minute later, Mike's head came up. He was suddenly
"Mike" again, pumped and ready to push on. A collective sigh
of relief passed through the floor.

Mike called a company-wide meeting. When the meeting
started, he shared a new vision. He said that Tellme would pivot
from the consumer market to corporate customers. He was confident and energized they would succeed. Everyone in the room
felt Mike's enthusiasm. They left the meeting feeling equally
pumped and energized to execute the vision.

Tellme secured their first 10 corporate accounts. Then 100
accounts. Mike's vision turned the company around. Years later,
the company was sold to Microsoft for nearly $800 million.

When things go sideways, fear flows in. Fear shrinks our
perspective down to the immediate threat. Fear steals our
power. Every employee at Tellme wondered whether they
could weather the storm, whether they would even have a job
in the coming months. Mike felt this threat himself. But almost
instinctively, he raised his head and focused on a plan of action
that would lead them through the tempest. Mike became the
guiding light.

Visions allow us to see beyond the threats of the present.
Great visionaries "reframe obstacles and threats as challenges
and opportunities."[29] Visionaries literally empower the group by
shifting their mindset from fear to reward. When the perspective
evolves, the problems dissolve. And when we think abstractly, we
are more likely to focus on the future. Thinking about the future
elicits more positive thoughts than thinking about the present.[30]
As pastor Rick Warren knows, the shepherd's job is not to simply watch the flock when the sun shines, it is to lead the flock
through troubled times to find the light.

Make a Million-Dollar Pitch

Startup pitches are high stakes moments that make or break dreams. When raising money, clear communication is not the goal. Entrepreneurs must show that they have a lucrative investment opportunity. If a pitch is crystal clear but lacks value, investors won't bite. When a pitch communicates value, even in the absence of clarity, investors take time to learn more. Value is the name of the game. But it's not the only game.

Laura Huang conducted research at Harvard to understand whether abstract language influenced the success of startup pitches.[31] She wanted to explore what steps women can take to overcome the gender gap in the investment world. Men are more than twice as likely to get funded than women. Previous research suggested that women tend to use more concrete language than men for a variety of reasons unrelated to power.[32] For example, concrete language is considered more relational and brings people closer together. Was language style a reason men were getting more money? Across three studies, Laura and her colleagues explored language differences in pitches.

In the first study, Laura and her colleagues found that men used more abstract language compared to women when pitching. This confirmed prior research that women sometimes speak more concretely. In the second study, Laura found that pitches using more abstract language were more likely to get funded. Abstract language was considered more visionary by investors. The visionary language generally led to higher perceptions of future growth.* Conversely, concrete language focused on existing performance. As one investor remarked, "I see men pitch unicorns and women pitch businesses."

---

*In my analysis of contest-winning pitches at TechCrunch Disrupt, one of the largest startup conferences in the world, over 70% of winners started or ended their pitch with a vision.[41]

But another interesting finding emerged. Speaking abstractly led to more investment regardless of whether it implied future growth or not. Laura and her colleagues speculated that a second reason abstract language was successful was because it signaled greater personal power in the speaker. In the third and final study, Laura found that when women used more abstract language in their pitches, it significantly improved perceptions of investment worthiness.

When you step into a meeting, do you begin with the big picture? As conversation unfolds, do you stay focused on the wider goals and vision?

The greatest leaders live a top-down life and see the forest from the trees. Your power is in your perspective. Whether your view comes through your goals, your values, or even your religion, connect to your power by focusing on the big picture. Your ability to see the big picture allows you to navigate the world without grinding away in the weeds.

See every step in life, every year, every career shift as part of a larger flow. Viewed from this perspective, even the steps that feel hard or backwards reveal themselves as forward movement. By understanding how to communicate value and by focusing on the big picture, you are now ready to explore power dynamics and coordination in teams.

The Power of Abstract Thinking

Powerful people see the big picture. When you tune your awareness to see the big picture, you engage your personal power.

What is a goal you want to pursue? The goal could be anything. Maybe you want to improve your health, to help others, to create something new, or to enhance your influence.

Once you have a clear goal, ask yourself why you want to pursue this goal in your life. For example, if your goal is to exercise weekly, answer the question "why do you want to exercise weekly?" Once you come up with an answer, ask yourself why again, then again, and one final time. In total, ask yourself "why" four times, progressing step-by-step until you arrive at a final reason.[42]

Your goal might be, "I want to exercise weekly." Why do you want to exercise weekly? "Because I want to be healthy." Why do you want to be healthy? "Because I want to feel good about myself." Why do you want to feel good about yourself? "Because then I feel more confident and can get more done." Why do you want to feel confident and get more done? "Because I want to live a successful and happy life."

Notice how each why-question progressively leads to a more abstract response, directing your thoughts into a wider and more abstract frame of thinking. When you take time to move through this exercise deliberately, research suggests you will experience a greater sense of control and feel more comfortable taking on a leadership role.[43] Make your responses meaningful to you. Your purpose is to dive deeper into yourself through answering why.

(continued)

(continued)

Make it a habit. Consider setting aside time each week to reflect on your goals and the overarching direction you will take your life in the following week. I do this regularly. Like the captain of a ship, when you pull out the map and remind yourself where you're going, you fit the daily and weekly activities into the larger vision you have for your life.

5 | Ringlead

Nancy was confident in her leadership but nervous about the CEO's drop-in visit. The company's new medical device was on track to receive government approval. Nancy led weekly meetings to tackle the FDA's ongoing requests. This meeting was a review of the latest requests. There was nothing unusual to warrant the CEO's presence.

Nancy ran her hand through her black hair as she reviewed one of the requests, then she asked for feedback from the room. Given that FDA approval was the gating factor to product release, she considered the possibility that the CEO was there to ensure things were on track.

As Nancy wrapped up the current request and readied herself to cover the next one, the CEO interrupted. Nancy swiveled her gaze to meet his. The CEO asked for an update about a side project related to product documentation. The side project had nothing to do with the FDA. Nancy was dumbstruck by the gear shift. Was there a connection she didn't see? Was the CEO upset about something? She only had a short time left to cover the remaining FDA requests. The CEO's non-trivial question required a long answer that would derail the meeting.

Responding to the FDA was without doubt the more important goal, but he was the CEO. Should she dodge the CEO's question or respond to his inquiry? Her mind raced.

How would you respond to the CEO in Nancy's shoes? Would you stay focused on the agenda or answer the question?

At Apple, clashes with CEOs are the stuff of legend. In Apple's early days, Steve Jobs was already legendary. He designed the first personal computer, then the Mac. But he was a young man. His leadership was immature. During meetings, he dominated conversation. His scathing criticisms were the stuff of Hollywood drama. Steve's autocratic style was one reason Apple's Board of Directors decided the company needed a more mature CEO. At the behest of the Board, Steve recruited John Sculley to take the reins of Apple. Steve worked under John, but the two had disagreements. A few years later, Steve engaged in a power struggle with John over who should lead the company.

The struggle led to Steve leaving Apple in disgrace.[1]

This isn't the only headline when an Apple executive crossed the CEO. The first iPhone was released in 2007. The phone came with Google Maps preinstalled. Google remained the default maps app on the iPhone for years. In 2012, Apple designed their own Maps app to replace Google. The initial release of Apple Maps was a disaster. The app was littered with bugs. Customers were furious. The stumbled launch was led by Scott Forstall, Senior VP of iPhone Software. Scott was a favorite of Steve Jobs, and many referred to Scott as a mini-Steve for his domineering leadership style. But Steve had recently passed away. The burden of managing the debacle fell on the shoulders of newly-minted CEO Tim Cook. To repair the relationship with the public, Tim asked Scott to publicly apologize for the poor service.

Scott believed an apology was unnecessary. He refused Tim's request.

Tim promptly fired Scott and issued the apology himself.[2]

If we put ourselves back in Nancy's shoes, what do we do when the CEO interrupts our meeting to ask a question? The correct response is to answer it!

Or is this the right response?

The challenge here is that we have two models of behavior clashing. Our default thinking tells us to submit to those above us. It's a no-brainer to avoid conflict with those above you. Your relationship with your superior is the key to your growth in an organization. When you cross the CEO, you run the risk of damaging your most important professional relationship. You also undermine the chain of command that allows groups to operate effectively.

But powerful people are internally driven. They don't blindly react to others. And powerful people add value. If Nancy took time to answer the CEO's question, it could negatively impact her negotiations with the FDA. In the long run a stumble with the FDA could tarnish her reputation with the CEO. Her options were therefore either to risk damaging her relationship with the CEO now or in the future.

We are not yet ready to understand how Nancy should navigate this challenge. First let's take a huge step back and explore how group interactions affect our status.

Status Roles in Teams

One of my all-time favorite research investigations was performed by David Owens.[3] David explored how individuals gain or lose status in corporate divisions. He found an R&D division in California that had one of the most progressive management systems of all time, *no formal titles and no formal reporting structure.* The division's purpose was to invent new products. The lack of structure inspired innovation. The division consisted of 120 employees with various backgrounds across engineering and science. Everyone basically did whatever they wanted, and reported to no one.

The division centered around projects. There were roughly 20 projects going on at any one time. The only corporate policy was that every employee had to participate in at least two projects. Individuals signed onto existing projects that interested them or proposed new project ideas. Those who proposed a project idea became project facilitators, but they had no formal power over other members on the team. Project teams self-organized.

David spent a year observing the R&D division. He visited the office several times a week, spoke with team members, and attended meetings. The lack of formal structure provided David the optimal environment to explore the behaviors of individuals in the absence of a fixed hierarchy.

When David began his research, he noticed immediately that informal hierarchies existed. Some people commanded more status than others. Those with high status had the best offices, the best equipment, and their voices carried the most weight. But why did some people have more status? They didn't start out with a better title or a higher position. What did they do differently that made them popular and powerful?

David discovered that status could be gained or lost primarily in group settings. Meetings. Meetings were an opportunity for the group to see how employees interacted with each other. These interactions conveyed each member's status. David identified three categories of unique behaviors during meetings – the behaviors of low status, medium status, and high status employees.

Low status employees focused on achieving a sense of belonging during meetings. They sought to fit in by flattering others. They acquiesced to avoid conflict. They performed menial tasks such as making handouts for the team. Low status behavior was particularly prevalent among new employees. New employees often sought to integrate with the group before building their reputation. And these behaviors successfully led to integration, but they also ensured new employees entered at the bottom of the hierarchy. It takes a long time to climb the ladder when you start at the bottom.

Medium status employees focused on communicating value toward the team's goals. They addressed problems. They readily engaged in debates on the best solutions. They promoted their credibility. In addition, medium status employees spoke up nearly twice as often as low status. This is what we expect when group value is measured by contribution.

Employees with the highest status communicated value, but they also did something different. David watched high status employees closely. He noticed that they controlled the flow of communication. They directed the conversation. They evaluated ideas. They summarized discussions. High status employees were operating not just as a cog in a machine but directing the machine itself. As a result, they were seen as more valuable to the team and more responsible for the team's success than their medium status colleagues. In addition, high status employees spoke up nearly twice as often as those with medium status.

In summary, those with the least status acquiesced to fit in, those with medium status added value, and those with the most status directed the conversation. It's worth noting that although low status employees ingratiated themselves more often than others, they spent nearly half their time communicating value. Likewise high status employees directed the conversation more often than others, but they still spent roughly 20% of their time contributing to a sense of belonging in order to foster group cohesion. Everyone from the lowest status to the highest communicated across this spectrum. The primary difference between levels of status was the distribution of how each employee spent their time. High status employees spent more time as ringleaders.

Be a Ringleader

After Steve Jobs' clash with CEO John Sculley and subsequent exit from Apple in 1984, Steve spent months reflecting on his behavior. That same year he formed a new venture, NeXT

Computer. Steve led the first all-hands meeting with NeXT's 11 employees in Pebble Beach, California. The team congregated in a spacious beige-walled room filled with sunlight to discuss the launch strategy for their first product.[4]

Steve spent most of the time in front of the room directing the discussion. He moved through the day's agenda, introducing each topic and eliciting comments from those in the room. Steve was the ringleader. He stood next to a whiteboard where he wrote down the group's ideas. Steve would later gain a reputation for working whiteboards during meetings. When the conversation deviated off topic, Steve interrupted to bring the group back on topic.

Ringleaders are given high status because they manage the agenda. The agenda supports the big picture goal. When you specify a goal and stick to an agenda, you maximize group effectiveness. The group is motivated to follow your agenda because they are motivated to achieve the goal. Goal focus secures status.

David Owens observed the same behavior in his status research – high status people tended to take on the role of "encouraging or constraining the participation"[5] of others. This behavior refocused conversation back to the agenda. Steve's behavior in the NeXT all-hands meeting was a far cry from the ego-centric reputation that plagued him at Apple only months before. Although Steve would always be known for being a dominator, more and more his leadership style focused on coordinating group activity toward a shared goal rather than his own ego.

Shine the Spotlight

Imagine you create a new public transportation system for your community. You join a group of community volunteers to discuss bus routes for your neighborhood. Each of you has your own ideas for routes. You spend a good chunk of your day working together to hash out a proposal. After a long discussion, you arrive at the perfect plan. You hand your proposal over to the city council. The city council takes your proposal and tosses it into the trash without a second glance.

This is exactly how I teach power to my university students.

During a mid-semester class, I invite students to design a hypothetical transportation system for the university. Students break into random teams of five and work together to come up with a new system. Each student has their own priorities. After toiling on details for 45 minutes, they hand their proposals over to me. Their faces shine with pride.

Then I hand each student a questionnaire. The questionnaire asks who contributed the most to the proposal and who had the most influence on the team. The questionnaire also asks students to rank order the status of each team member. Students dutifully fill out the short questionnaire. Then I tell them I don't care about their transportation plans, this was a field test on group power dynamics. Surprise! The disappointment on their faces fills me with warmth for what's coming. Together we go over the results of the questionnaire.

Do status differences show up in groups during their brief time working together? The answer is yes. In less than an hour, status structures form.* Is there general agreement about each person's status in the group? The answer is yes. Everyone agrees who is on top and who is on bottom. They feel it.

Next, we reflect on the behaviors that contributed to status. This reflection allows students to connect their feelings of status with the behaviors they witnessed. As students reflect, the disappointment on their faces transforms to wisdom in their eyes. Remarkably, status behaviors are clear and consistent across groups.

What behaviors do students witness by those with the highest status?

---

*I've run this exercise in as little as 15 minutes with similar results.

Students who achieved the most status oriented the group toward the group's goal. They were the ringleaders. Ringleaders often instinctively grabbed the whiteboard marker and led the conversation from the board. Controlling the whiteboard was a huge power move. Ringleaders encouraged others to speak and wrote down ideas.* Then the ringleaders validated what others shared, and they synthesized those ideas into the wider frame of the discussion. Everyone's attention was on the ringleader because the ringleader directed everyone's attention across the group.

Students with the lowest status either failed to frequently contribute ideas or they distanced themselves from group discussion. One time I watched two students split off from their team to discuss an idea between themselves. The two students thought their idea had potential and wanted to give it extra attention before bringing it up to the group. Even though they later reintegrated and shared their thoughts, the long separation from the center of discussion put both of them at the bottom of the status hierarchy.

Thus we come to one of the most important concepts in power dynamics, what I call the *spotlight principle*. Take two people, one standing in the spotlight and the other standing in shadow. Who has the most power in that room, the one in the light or the one in the dark?

The answer is neither. This is a trick question. The one with the most power in the room is the third person who controls the spotlight.

ExxonMobil CEO Rex Tillerson was known to run senior review meetings following the 90/10 rule, 90% listening and 10% speaking. First he listened to everyone share their updates. He focused on each speaker, giving them his full attention. To senior staff, it felt like Rex was an "intellectual judge." If Rex

---

*Controlling the whiteboard is completely different from taking meeting minutes in the back corner. Ringleading is active engagement, whereas taking meeting minutes is passive.

had reservations, he held onto them as he listened. Non-reactive. Toward the end of the meeting, Rex would step back and identify the three key issues to address based on the discussion. This was his role. Rex synthesized ideas. In a meeting filled with disparate ideas, your ability to elicit feedback and then synthesize the group's thoughts delivers value.

You don't have to be the smartest person in the room to gain status. One of the best roles you can take during a meeting is to elicit opinions from others. When you are not qualified to take a stand on the subject, be neither for nor against a position. Instead, elicit opinions from those who are qualified. By no means does this require you to dominate the conversation. Quite the opposite. The path to status is sometimes stepping out of the contributor role and into the coordinator role. When you control the flow of conversation, you make room for everyone to share their ideas. This empowers you into the conversation by coordinating the sharing. And incidentally, it is often the coordinator who ends up speaking more overall than any single contributor.

As we move into an age of vigilant inclusion, the value of the coordinator role has only increased. You can enhance your power as a coordinator by supporting the voices of those who struggle to be heard. Half of my clients are women who face the challenge of being frequently interrupted.*When you witness someone get interrupted for no clear reason, regardless of whether it's a woman, a man, or a minority, speak up. Tell the person who interrupted that you want to hear the previous speaker finish their thoughts. If someone tries to dominate the conversation or doesn't add value, you can direct the

---

*When you allow yourself to be interrupted and pulled off topic by someone who knows less than you, you not only hinder yourself, you hinder the group. If someone interrupts you, ignore the interruption and finish your sentence. Finishing sentences shows non-reaction. Once you finish your sentence, you can listen to what the other person has to say. Or if the interruption is off topic, you can continue speaking without acknowledging the interruption.

spotlight back to those who do add value. You do a service to both inclusion and your group's goal by protecting participation. Those protected will feel valued. And your influence on conversation flow is interpreted as powerful by everyone in the group, including the person you corrected. You will feel that power course through your veins as well. We call it a sense of control.

The Greater Good is Ratified

The executive operations team at Apple convened to discuss challenges facing the company in Asia. Then-COO Tim Cook and his top lieutenants gathered in a conference room where they reviewed a host of ongoing concerns. At one point in the discussion while addressing a particular issue, Tim looked over at VP Sabih Kahn. "Someone should be in China driving this," Tim said.[6] Sabih nodded and the conversation continued. Thirty minutes later, Tim looked at Sabih again. Then Tim abruptly asked, "why are you still here?" Sabih immediately left the meeting and drove to the airport without packing. He caught the first flight out to China that afternoon.

If you want power in groups, others must ratify your status. Ratification means others respond to your direction. Every time you refocus the group on the agenda, every time you invite others to speak, you direct the group. When others respond to your direction, they ratify and strengthen your status in the group.[7]

One of the most effective ways to ratify your status in groups is to assign tasks. As ringleader, you are uniquely situated to see the big picture. You can call on others to take up roles and responsibilities toward the larger goal. When you assign tasks toward a shared goal, others are motivated to follow. When others follow, they ratify your status and a healthy power dynamic is created.

In the Apple operations meeting, when Sabih responded to Tim's assignment, Sabih ratified Tim's status as the leader. Years later Sabih was promoted to Senior VP. The move was partially explained as a result of Sabih's loyalty. Tim knew how to lead, and Sabih knew how to follow.

But what happens when employees don't follow directions? We witnessed the result when Apple VP Scott Forstall refused Tim Cook's request to apologize for the Apple Maps debacle in 2012. Previously Scott and Tim had been peers. But Tim was recently promoted to CEO and establishing his newfound authority. Scott's refusal challenged Tim's authority. Tim fired Scott as a result. Had Tim not fired Scott, Tim's status at Apple could have diminished for allowing the challenge to stand.

If we want to effectively challenge leaders, it's not by following in the footsteps of Scott Forstall. When Scott refused to apologize, his behavior was largely seen as self-serving. The refusal was a challenge to Tim's status, not a focus on the success of the corporation.

Kirsten Keller researched power conflicts in the workplace.[8] She discovered that power conflicts show up predominantly as peers or supervisors attempting to dominate others. For example, one of my colleagues witnessed a VP turn to a junior employee during a corporate meeting and say, "you know I could fire you right now if I wanted to." Everybody in the room did a double take. Kirsten observed that those who initiate power conflicts such as overt domineering like this VP are perceived as driven by fear. Fear is the embodiment of a low-power mindset. When individuals attempt to ratify their power through random acts of dominance, or when they refuse others through random acts of resistance, Kirsten's research suggests that others sense the weakness hidden behind the bluster. Such conflicts inevitably lead to negative emotions and hinder team performance.* Perhaps even worse, when we seek

---

*Forty-seven percent of group conflicts focus on power.[16] Power conflicts reduce information sharing because they lead people to withdraw from the conversation or lead people to be ignored.

respect through overt status challenges, we are seeking validation. Seeking validation is a low-power mindset. Externally we
may temporarily create the illusion of power, but internally we
create a wasteland of powerlessness. This approach to power is
not sustainable.

There is no point to "win" the most power in a group. You're
operating together. You might compete to ensure your idea is
heard, but otherwise it's not a competition. Personal power is
a way of being, not a way of being on top. If someone wields
power over you for the good of the group, great! The best value
you can add is to go along with it. This isn't a contest for who's
top dog, this is a commitment to creating group value. Serving
the group is your pathway to enhancing your status at whatever
level you are at.

Effective power negotiations don't appear as conflicts at
all. These negotiations appear as a refocus on the bigger picture and implementation of important goals. In fact, powerful
people often act as the peacekeepers of a group to maintain
the group's structure.[9] Status ratification isn't a path to power,
it's a result. Your success in coordinating activity occurs when
you focus on the needs of the group. The degree to which
others respond to you is the degree to which they view you as
serving their needs. And if others don't respond to you, it's an
opportunity to learn and readjust. You don't have to be nice.
You don't have to be gentle. But you do have to be focused on
delivering value.

Back to the initial question at the beginning of the chapter,
can we challenge superiors effectively?

Nancy stood at the front of the meeting room. She needed
to focus on FDA approval, but the CEO's off-topic question rang
in her ears. Should she maintain the meeting agenda or appease
the CEO's errant curiosity? After a pause, her brain kicked back
into gear. Responding to the FDA was without question the
more important goal. Nancy hesitated a moment longer, then she

looked at the CEO and said, "that's a great question. Let's focus on addressing the FDA's concerns first to ensure regulatory approval. I'll give you a full status report after the meeting." Nancy's chest tightened as she waited for a response. The CEO nodded. Sweating, Nancy proceeded to the next point on her checklist.

When the meeting ended and everyone adjourned, the CEO walked straight up to Nancy. She stared at him silently, fearing the worst. His brow furled with a strange twist. Then he apologized for interrupting her. She was again dumbstruck! She also felt herself stand a little straighter. Her status with the CEO had apparently just risen. It would continue to rise in the following months.

The best way to challenge a leader is to ensure our actions are made for the benefit of the leader. The objective is not to challenge the leader's status, it is to support the leader and the group.[10] Nancy did not challenge the CEO's status. Instead she communicated three qualities – that she was focused on the goal, that she would not react and lose focus, and her ability to stay focused showed she was capable of coordinating the group in service to the goal.

Power is not fundamentally in the command, it is in value to the group. Coordinating the group toward a shared goal sanctions your right as the leader to lead. And when you successfully coordinate group activity, you enhance your personal power because you experience a sense of control in your environment.

Empower Others

Carol led worldwide sales operations for a technology company. She was a hands-off manager who greeted employees with a wide smile and laughed frequently. But her employees regarded her with respect not for her attitude, but for her leadership style. Carol led like a military general. Nothing so grossly Hollywood like barking orders. No, Carol practiced Commander's Intent.

Commander's Intent empowers teams to achieve goals in the face of uncertainty. The U.S. Military introduced Commander's Intent at the twilight of the 19th century, and the concept has continued to gain support since then. Today Commander's Intent plays a vital role in 21st century military operation. Commander's Intent is defined as "a concise statement of the purpose . . . to focus subordinates on what has to be accomplished in order to achieve success, even when the plan and concept no longer apply."[11] Let's take a look at what that means.

Just as leaders are keepers of a vision, they are drivers of goals.[12] Goals implement visions. Carol's vision was to strategically reposition her organization to be more competitive in the market. At an otherwise high-tech company, communication consisted of passing physical notes between departments to keep track of customers. The company literally operated on sticky notes. To fulfill her vision, Carol set the goal to update inter-department communication technology.

Carol charged Lauren to implement a new platform integrating communication across departments. Lauren was a low-level manager on Carol's team. Carol provided Lauren the information to get started and then let Lauren take over. And this is where Carol's leadership style shined.

The U.S. Military identified four equally important steps to the process of Commander's Intent. The senior commander (1) formulates and (2) communicates an abstract goal. When leaders communicate relatively abstract goals, it provides subordinates the freedom to employ creative solutions. The subordinate commander (3) interprets the goal and (4) ensures it gets done. In simple terms, senior leaders focus on big pictures and subordinate leaders focus on action plans. Together, the two command levels execute orders that drive military success.

Carol communicated the need for an integrated platform but didn't instruct Lauren on how to implement it. Lauren was responsible for interpreting and implementing the goal. This gave Lauren the freedom to test various implementation strategies to get the job done.

The military found that communicating abstract goals without a concrete execution plan motivates subordinates to take responsibility and employ creative solutions. Creativity in turn promotes self-efficacy. Therefore, when leaders communicate abstract goals, not only is their abstract language viewed as powerful, their language empowers others.

Lauren took to her new responsibility immediately. She recruited a team to drive adoption of the new platform across the various departments. But because Lauren was a low-level manager, she ran into a problem. Even after recruiting a team and assigning tasks, no one listened to her. The project was going nowhere.

When David Owens studied status behaviors in corporations, he noted that high status people reinforced stability and order among employees during meetings. Carol understood power, so Carol sat in on Lauren's team meetings. Because Carol had authority in the company, employees in the meeting asked Carol what to do. Carol pointed to Lauren and said, *this is what Lauren tells me. Here's what she needs to get the job done.* Carol then handed the floor to Lauren. When stakeholders rang Carol outside meetings, Carol told them to stop coming to her and start going to Lauren, whom she had put in charge of the project. Shortly after Lauren received Carol's endorsement, employees across divisions began responding to Lauren's task assignments. Carol's endorsement not only empowered Lauren, it reinforced Carol's own status by maintaining order.

It behooves leaders to empower their subordinates to implement goals. Senior leaders manage large projects. Leaders may be able to take on multiple aspects of a project themselves, but they have neither the time nor the expertise to take on every role. Delegation is power. Among Stanford Business School alumni, there is a saying that when MBAs enter the workforce, their ambition drives them to do great things. But after a few short years, many of them take on too much responsibility and burn out. After burn-out, the MBAs "either learn to delegate or become yoga teachers." As Head of Worldwide Sales Operations, Carol delegated projects to her team and empowered them to achieve those projects. Carol understood the psychology of status and personal power.

Within months, the company had a new streamlined customer management platform. The platform increased the company's competitiveness in the market. Carol's actions also won Lauren's trust. Lauren became comfortable sharing new ideas. The addi-tional information Lauren shared with Carol reinforced Carol's power within the organization.

Build Trust

Linh had been in the consulting industry for over 10 years. She was the type of woman who walked into job interviews demand-ing twice her previous salary. And got it. She learned how to be strong from her mother, who raised her during a period of fam-ine in Vietnam. Linh immigrated to North America for college. She carried her childhood lessons with her, launching her career on a vertical trajectory. Now working at Accenture, her team was brought in to support a new client. The client's productivity was way down, and radical change was required.

Linh began to shape a new culture for the client to allow transformation to take place. But the transformation was stress-ful, and the client's stress led to short tempers and sharp criti-cisms against Linh's team. Her team began blaming each other behind closed doors for the disintegrating client relationship.

One employee, Sam, spoke up first at their latest internal meeting, "I met with the client today and told him he needs to respect my team."

John immediately snapped back, "Your team? You mean our team."

Sam retorted that he was the one doing the most work, and John's ideas were continually failing. The meeting was a mess. Everyone was taking things personally and blame was the name of the game.

Linh interrupted the foray. "Here's what I'm hearing from you Sam. You tried hard, you did a good job. The client didn't appreciate it." Sam nodded. She turned to John, "you were right setting up the system you did. That was a good move, but the client rejected it." John sighed and released the tension in his shoulders. With both her teammates now listening, Linh recentered the agenda on objective positives and negatives so the team could move forward. For the rest of the meeting, the team dropped the blame and focused on the goals.

People are hungry for validation. Linh understood that ultimately her team wanted to be heard and validated. Rather than lead with criticism, she acknowledged their work and refocused the discussion on action. Doing so created a level of trust and safety that led to an effective meeting outcome.

Status reputations are built on trust. Shawn Burke and his colleagues conducted a meta-study on trust in leadership, basically a review of all the research ever done around leadership trust.[13] They discovered that trust was built on three components – trust in the leader's ability; trust in the leader's benevolence; and trust in the leader's integrity. Trust in ability centered around the leader's capability to create structure within the team and set a clear compelling direction. Trust in benevolence involved empowering team members and allowing them to voice their opinions around important decisions. Trust in integrity centered around consistency to valued principles, accepting responsibility, and holding others accountable. Is there any surprise that many of the facets of trust overlap with personal power?*

---

*Trust also enhances the perceived value of your contributions, meaning the more others trust you, the more your contributions are valued.[17]

John Mackey, CEO and founder of Whole Foods, regularly toured the grocery store floors of his business. He had a larger-than-life presence to employees. John said the effect was that, "I can give 10 compliments [to employees], but the one criticism devastates the morale."[14] He confided that he would share problems with store managers, but generally avoid personal criticisms. "In my experience, criticism will only be received by people if there's a high degree of trust. If there's trust, and people know that you care about them, then their self-esteem is less threatened." John understood that trust is key to leading others.

No One is Off the Hook

Steve panicked. It was 8am in downtown Boston and the copy center hadn't finished printing his proposal. Twelve fat binders of documents needed to be copied and hand-delivered to the United States Navy by exactly noon. The Navy had put out a call for proposals to deploy new underwater equipment. The contract was worth a handsome $50 million dollars. Steve arrived in Boston the night before lugging his payload from his office in New York.

But the printers at the copy center were offline. The system failed that morning while printing the five requisite copies required by the Navy – a total of 60 binders. Steve waited. His wool suit itched as he watched a technician work on the system. Copy center employees shuffled back and forth. Then Steve heard the beautiful sound of printers warming up and spitting out paper. He checked his watch. It was now 10am.

When the Navy first issued a call for proposals, Steve's president saw an opportunity for their equipment company to expand. The company had served the oil and gas industry for years. But the energy market had matured. The company needed to enter a new market for growth. The president delegated Steve, a mid-level manager, to submit a proposal to the Navy. Steve organized a team for the task. Over six weeks, Steve and his team produced the 12 fat binders of material outlining their plan.

The print finished. Steve grabbed the binders and swooped into his car. He slammed the pedal to the metal racing toward the Naval office. Then he hit traffic on the bridge. His car crawled. A two-minute stretch of road turned into 30 minutes. When traffic let up, Steve floored it.

Steve arrived at the Naval office. He rushed in and dropped the binders on the front desk. The officer at the front casually looked at the binders. Then the officer looked up at the clock. It was 12:02pm. The officer looked at Steve. Steve was told that the deadline was 12:00, not 12:02pm.

The proposal was rejected.

What should have been a career win for Steve suddenly transformed into the worst day of his life. Steve spent several minutes begging, cajoling, and trying to persuade the officer. No luck. Steve left the office with his head hung low. He drove back to his hotel. Then he worked up the courage to call the company president.

The president was livid. He screamed through the phone. He demanded to know why Steve hadn't called earlier to ask for assistance. When the president hung up, Steve packed his bags and dragged himself to the airport. He caught the gloomy flight home.

Steve arrived at his office later that afternoon. The president called a meeting. The first thing the president did was take personal responsibility for the failure. Then the president told Steve and his team that they were equally accountable for failing to avert the disaster. The president issued a 10% salary cut to everyone on the team, including the president himself, until the team got a new contract with the Navy. It was indeed a bad day.

Holding the team accountable seems like a just punishment for failure. Steve lost out on a $50 million opportunity. If anything, a 10% salary cut sounds magnanimous. And punishment is a tool that reinforces one's authority. Punishment demonstrated the president's formal power. But holding others accountable has a deeper purpose than propping up one's formal power through punishment.

Holding others accountable demonstrates your personal power. Rooted in a sense of control, you expect others to take responsibility, thereby conveying your high-power mindset.[15] And accountability empowers others. When others are held accountable, it acknowledges their responsibility over the situation and breaks the illusion of powerlessness.* In addition, tasks are for the benefit of the group. When someone fails to implement their task, the group fails. Whether you have formal power to punish or not, when you hold someone accountable, you stand for the group. You signal your ability to serve the group and build trust that you can manage others toward the goal. Even holding others verbally accountable is sufficient. When others respond to you, your actions are ratified. Thus, holding others accountable enhances both your personal power and that of the group.

Three months passed. Steve's team suffered the 10% salary cut. They tightened their personal budgets. They ate out less. Finally, Steve closed a nominal $5000 contract with the Navy. The president honored his word and reinstated full salaries to everyone. The disaster had passed.

Engage the Group

Greg was expanding his startup's marketing footprint. His business had grown to over 100 employees and could hardly be called a startup now. Greg believed their brand needed a more professional look, so he engaged the marketing team to brainstorm new logo designs. He and the team had been meeting weekly to discuss the new logo for over a month now.

Greg smiled as he sat in the current meeting. The team reviewed their recent progress. It was a fruitful conversation. Midway through the meeting, the VP of Marketing strolled

---

*This is why organizations that support accountability create cultures of empowerment.

in. Everyone looked up. It was the first time the VP had attended one of the design meetings. A few weeks prior, Greg's cofounder had hired the new VP of Marketing. Greg found it a bit strange that the VP hadn't participated in these logo meetings, but the VP was new and Greg didn't think much of it.

The VP strolled to the center of the room and slapped a logo down on the conference table. "This will be our new design," he said. Everyone squinted to look. The logo image was reminiscent of a nuclear bomb, not dissimilar to the way the VP just dropped it on the team. The VP had been working on a logo design by himself the last few days. He didn't want to share the news until he was ready to unveil his work. What the VP didn't realize was that a similar logo had been reviewed and unanimously rejected weeks ago.

The marketing team stared at the logo. In silence, the team turned to Greg. Greg raised an eyebrow and turned to the VP. Greg then explained that a similar idea had already been evaluated. The VP sputtered and began defending his idea, but the entire marketing team filed behind Greg and voiced criticisms of the design. The logo was rejected. The VP's neglect to engage the group damaged his status debut at the outset. What the VP should have done was take on the role of coordinator in the discussions.

When we go it alone, our actions are invisible to the interplay of power dynamics. Power is power in social groups. The group is greater than the individual. Your ability to coordinate group activity adds more value to the group than your individual contributions. You don't need to be the smartest person in the room to demonstrate power, you simply need to lead the agenda and make space for other voices to be heard. Nor do you need to do all the work. When you assign tasks, empower others, and hold them accountable, you strengthen your contribution to the group and build trust in the process.

Personal power by definition is not a zero-sum game. Personal power is an experience we ourselves own. And many of our powerful behaviors empower others. The powerful help others see the big picture. The powerful bring others into the spotlight. The powerful facilitate others' sense of control through delegation and accountability. Personal power enhances ourselves, and it is the team as a whole that is empowered as a result.

But you will be challenged. You will be taken advantage of. How you maintain respect in these situations and avoid being treated poorly is what we cover in the following chapters.

The Power of Taking on Responsibility

In order to be a ringleader, you need to manage the agenda and direct the conversation. But if you don't already feel powerful, taking that first step can be hard.

It's not hard to think about being in charge. We're in charge of situations all the time, from running projects to making group decisions to evaluating the work of others. When we think about managing even a simple group task, the power circuits in our brain light up.

Before you step into a meeting that you want to run, consider the goals of the meeting. Now consider how you can structure the agenda to achieve those goals. Thinking about this process, choose which responsibilities you aim to take on. You can choose to moderate the discussion. You can choose to actively participate in making decisions. You can choose the standards used to evaluate the quality of ideas.[18] Acknowledge the importance of your responsibilities toward achieving the goal.

By thinking about the meeting and making the conscious decision to involve yourself in certain responsibilities, you tap into your personal power and ready yourself to engage. Those in the meeting may welcome your engagement because pursuing an agenda and taking on responsibilities reduces the burden of responsibility on everyone else.

PART III

Taking

6

Set Boundaries

Sarah stepped into her performance review ready for her promotion. She was a director at one of the most prestigious organizations in the world, excelling at everything she touched. Her colleagues saw her as a confident leader who cut to the chase. When she ran meetings, things got done. She also made time to chat with employees about their lives. She lent a sympathetic ear to their challenges. She taught yoga on weekends.

Sarah had been with the organization for almost a decade. She was hired alongside two other hardworking colleagues. In recent years her two colleagues were promoted above her. They worked in different areas and she was the sole woman amongst them. She took it in stride. This job was her dream. She couldn't be happier doing what she was doing. Her team had carved out a set of key responsibilities within the organization. They achieved results. With her performance review, Sarah was finally going to have her moment.

Her executive manager smiled as he sat down across from her. He issued his congratulations. "Sarah, you did great work. You achieved outstanding results. In fact, you consistently outperform expectations." Sarah took it all in, feeling a glow in her chest. "Leadership values you. Your colleagues value you. You excel at your job. Everyone sees that."

Sarah did everything you learned in this book so far. She added value, she led teams. And she was recognized for her hard work.

The manager rubbed his chin, thoughtful for a moment. Then he continued. "You are dedicated to this organization and passionate about your work." He shrugged his shoulders. "And because you love your job we know that you won't leave. We're happy to have you where you are, so we see no reason to promote you right now."

Sarah's gut clenched. She stared back, unable to speak.

We've all been there. We give and others take. If power were all about giving, people pleasers would rule the world. But they don't. Delivering value is only half the equation. To grow in personal power, we must assert ourselves. The most important way to assert ourselves is through self-respect. But how do we practice self-respect?

Fairness

Maggie Neale wrote five books on negotiation and is one of the leading negotiation researchers in the country. Many of her research findings challenged traditional wisdom. For example, many people assume that you should let your partner make the first offer during a negotiation. Maggie's research showed the opposite - those who make the first offer walk away with more.[*,1] Halfway through her career, she had a high-profile job at Kellogg Graduate School of Management pursuing research

---

[*]The common misconception is that making the first offer results in sharing more information with the other party, thereby giving them an edge in the negotiation. However, making the first offer anchors the negotiation price more favorably by setting the starting point from which the other person will counter. Research also shows that those who feel more powerful are more likely to make the first offer. Thus again, we see an alignment between the inner psychology of power and the outer advantages of radiating power.

as well as training the next generation of faculty PhDs. Then Stanford reached out to recruit her for their business faculty. Maggie emailed Stanford her CV. Three years in a row. Finally she was asked to interview for a senior faculty position.

After the interview, the senior associate dean of Stanford's business school called to make Maggie an offer. When Stanford makes you an offer, you accept. In fact there is an unspoken pride among Stanford leadership that, *We're Stanford. If we ask you to join us, you will come.* And literally almost everybody does. Maggie knew this. Maggie had also done her homework. Before the dean's call, Maggie reached out to her colleagues at Stanford and other schools to inquire about typical compensation rates for faculty. It turned out the Stanford salaries were substantially lower than her current compensation.

As the dean prepared to make his initial salary offer over the phone, Maggie interrupted, "before we get started, I'm concerned you are going to make me an offer that is less than I'm making at Kellogg." Obviously, Maggie wasn't going to let someone else make the first offer. The dean paused, then inquired about her current salary at Kellogg. Maggie shared her faculty salary and other aspects of her compensation, then she proposed an offer that she felt was reasonable.

The dean harumphed. He exclaimed that her request was more in line with what accounting professors made, not organizational behavior professors like Maggie.

"Well, can accounting professors teach negotiation?" Maggie asked.

"Of course not," the dean replied.

"Well, they might have to, as I won't be," she countered.

And just like that Maggie made history. She became among the first few to decline a faculty job offer by Stanford's business school.

Researchers at UC Berkeley analyzed successful negotiation strategies, when to give, when to take, how to balance the two.[2] Their analysis outlined four phases. After the (1) initiation phase in which negotiators signal they are willing to cooperate, much like a handshake of trust, discussion begins in earnest. The (2) positioning phase is when negotiators compete to claim value for themselves. This phase is where each party asks for what they want. When claiming value begins to fail, negotiators switch to (3) creating value and problem-solving for one another. The (4) endgame phase returns to claiming value and securing promises. Successful negotiation is a dance between claiming value and creating value.

Maggie knew there were advantages to working at Stanford, but she didn't allow herself to get tunnel vision. Her life at Kellogg was great. She had a nice home, her family was settled, her job was secure, and her research and teaching opportunities were abundant. But the phone call with the dean wasn't over, and nobody wins with outright rejection. That was only phase 2.

Maggie explained to the dean why her compensation request was appropriate. Stanford sought someone who was both an outstanding researcher and teacher. Maggie fit the bill. Stanford focused on increasing the number of women faculty. Stanford PhDs also struggled to get jobs, and Maggie had a successful record supporting PhDs. Maggie shifted the conversation from a battle over dollars to the benefits she would bring to Stanford and the business school. Now she was in phase 3. The dean listened.

A week later the dean called back and offered Maggie a significantly higher salary.

Maggie accepted his offer. She spent the next twenty-five years at Stanford.

Sheryl Sandberg was the COO of Facebook for nearly 14 years. When Sheryl was initially offered the COO role, the compensation package provided by Mark Zuckerberg was excellent. And in Sheryl's own words she said, "I was afraid if I negotiated, [Mark] wouldn't want me. And he wouldn't like me."[3] But when Sheryl's brother-in-law told her a man would negotiate and get paid twice the salary, it struck a nerve. Money wasn't Sheryl's primary motivation, but fairness was. She decided to push back on the offer. When Sheryl met with Mark again, she said "you're hiring me to lead your negotiating teams. So this is the only time we'll ever be on the other side of the table. And I'm going to bring these skills to my job at Facebook. I know you would be disappointed if I didn't show you I had these skills."[4] Then Sheryl made her counteroffer. She danced between claiming value and creating value. And she received what she asked for.

Fairness is a key concept in personal power. Researchers paired college students together to play the ultimatum game.[5] In the ultimatum game, one student receives some money, a few dollars in this case. That student splits the money with their partner. Splits don't have to be an equal 50/50. For example, the splitter might decide to give 40% of the money to their partner and keep 60% for themselves. Or the splitter might only give 10% of the money to their partner and keep 90% for themselves. Their partner can either accept or reject the split. If the split is accepted, both people walk away with their money. If the split is refused, neither student walks away with any money. It's always in the interest of partners to accept offers, even unfair ones, because they walk away with some money. Even a little money is better than no money.

To see how personal power affects whether partners accept unfair offers, half of the partners were conditioned to experience higher personal power by affirming an important personal value. The other half were left unconditioned. How did personal power influence behavior? When partners were offered only 10–20% of the split, those who felt powerful accepted the offer roughly 15% of the time, whereas unconditioned partners accepted the offer 40% of the time. *Powerful people expect fair treatment*, and they are quick to reject unfair offers. Conversely, those with less personal power are more tolerant of unfairness.

One of my friends was extended a job offer during COVID. The employer searched for months to find a good fit for the role, and she was perfect. But the initial salary offer was way below market value. My friend confided in me that it would be hard as a single mom to take care of her child and make house payments with that salary. But she was even more scared of angering the hiring manager and losing the offer. Against my advice and out of fear, my friend accepted the lowball offer without negotiating. Reacting to fear is the essence of low personal power. She focused on what she had to lose, never stopping to consider what the employer had to lose by turning her down.* The mere fact she was at the negotiation table was already evidence that she was valuable to the other party.**

Chronic giving and capitulation are driven in part by the mistaken belief that our value is measured solely by what we give. *Power itself is an indicator of our value.* Displays of power signal our capacity to add value.[6] When we behave in ways that show self-respect, we show power. The more powerful we appear, the more value we appear to possess. When we demand fair compensation, we appear more valuable. It's that simple. Others may get upset when they run into our expectations. Sheryl Sandberg said she feared Mark Zuckerberg would like her less for negotiating. And when Sheryl pushed back on the salary, Mark was upset. But Sheryl maintained her boundaries despite her fear, and in doing so quickly became one of Mark's closest confidants.***

---

*Focusing on what we have to lose is loss aversion. Loss aversion suggests that the psychological pain of loss is twice as strong as the pleasure of reward.[23] Therefore, people focus more attention on what they have to lose rather than what they have to gain. Loss aversion is natural, but if you let it guide your actions, it keeps you playing small.

**An experienced HR representative told me that companies generally budget 20% extra over their initial offers so they have room to negotiate. The money is on the table waiting to be claimed. You run the risk of being less respected if you don't reach for it. You also lose out on an opportunity to bring home more money for your family.

***Research suggests that leaders are sensitive to arguments for fairness and more likely to adjust their behavior when subordinates provide feedback that leaders are being unfair. Conversely, when subordinates acquiesce to unfairness, leaders become increasingly self-interested. You dig a hole for yourself when you don't speak up for fairness.[24]

When we allow ourselves to be treated unfairly, we signal less power and therefore less value. Paradoxically, chronic giving can become the vehicle through which we are seen to have less to give. We may come off as desperate or needy. Whereas when we act with self-respect and give less, we are seen to have more to give.*

In addition, research shows that reciprocation isn't automatic in negotiations.[7] If you continually make concessions during a negotiation without claiming value, you never allow space for the other person to reciprocate. Chronic giving prevents the other person from reciprocating, not necessarily because they are selfish, but because they are not motivated to consider how to reciprocate. By over-giving, we prevent others from giving back. Thus a lack of self-respect becomes a self-fulfilling prophecy. A quote I once heard is that, "people will respect you to the level you respect yourself, and people will disrespect you to the level that you tolerate."[8]

I had a colleague who didn't claim her worth. She had been with her company for several years. As her accomplishments grew, she felt she deserved a raise. She dropped hints to management about a salary increase, but she never made a strong push for it. As a result, nothing changed. Reciprocation isn't automatic. Eventually her feelings of resentment overflowed and she handed in her resignation letter. Her manager was blindsided. He offered her a salary raise. He offered her more time off. But it was too late. Her resentment was too

---

*In negotiations, find your "no" level. Would you still want the job if they paid you minimum wage, or would you want a partnership if your partner doesn't reciprocate? There is always a boundary where you are unwilling to make the exchange. When you find your boundary, it becomes an anchor from which to practice self-respect. And when you practice self-respect, you gain more respect.

strong. She left her job and they lost her skills. Without self-respect, everybody loses.*

To live in your power, you must recognize the value you bring and own it. When you feel powerful, you will expect fair treatment and voice those desires.

At the beginning of the chapter, Sarah's performance review was supposed to be a victory celebration. Instead it turned into a nightmare. Sarah sat staring at her manager. His words rang in her ears, "Because you love your job we know that you won't leave. . . So we see no reason to promote you right now." And Sarah did love her job. She was doing exactly what she always wanted to do. But in that moment, her passion was not at the forefront of her mind. Her manager recognized her outstanding contributions. But he refused to reward her for them.

Sarah couldn't respond immediately because her body had clenched up. If her manager said more words after that, she didn't hear them. All Sarah felt was outrage over the unfair treatment. She paused for a time. When she finally found her breath, she looked her manager in the eye and responded in a neutral voice, "If this is the way I'm going to be treated here, then you're wrong to think I won't leave."

She got the promotion.

---

*Rather than resign, an effective approach is to speak with leadership. During the conversation, state that the current relationship is unequal, explain your contributions, and explore ways to achieve equality. This conversation should be approached as a negotiation, where both parties work together to claim and create value. Before having this conversation, it's also important to understand the value you contribute to the company. Fairness is not determined only by what you believe you deserve, but by the perceived value you bring to the group and what the group is capable of rewarding you for that value. Speak with your peers to evaluate whether you are being treated fairly. Be prepared to see both sides and to focus on fairness, rather than winning. With self-respect, everyone wins.

Respond (Don't React) to Threats

Tammie was a good person in a bad situation. She stood 5'2" and almost always wore a smile on her face. Tammie treated her colleagues like friends. She invited them over for coffee. She held dinner parties. But her manager was toxic. The boss spewed vitriol to employees. Daily emails of abuse were common. One-on-ones left Tammie in tears. Team meetings stung the most – no one was safe from the boss' abuse. The only solace Tammie took during meetings was the hope that the focus wouldn't fall on her. It still hurt to watch her teammates cut down.

Tammie lodged a complaint to HR. It's no secret that corporate HR works for leadership. Tammie was told that her manager's abuse was "within acceptable guidelines of behavior." In other words, the company valued the toxic boss more than Tammie's happiness. But the HR manager gave Tammie some personal advice on how to deal with the situation. In two simple words, the advice was *don't react.*

Tammie gave this advice a shot at the next team meeting. It took only a few minutes before the boss locked eyes with her. The boss started hurling aspersions at her performance. As insult after insult rained down, Tammie's pulse raced with anxiety on the inside. She felt throbbing in her eardrums. But on the outside, Tammie stared at the boss with a calm neutral expression. Her boss kept up the attack. And while everything in Tammie screamed to curl up and hide, she let the inner and outer noise flow over her like water. After a few minutes, the boss's spate of attacks died down. Tammie continued to look at the boss calmly. Eventually the boss stopped speaking all together. Tammie continued to say nothing. She kept her face completely passive. The silence stretched.

Then something unexpected happened. The boss looked away uncomfortably.

After that meeting, Tammie was never attacked again. I have heard this exact technique used successfully many times to confront office bullies.

High-power people act, and low-power people react. Reaction ratifies the action. One way people disrespect us is through verbal assaults. When we react to these verbal assaults through assent or defense, we ratify them. Whereas when we do not react, we do not ratify them. When Tammie did not react to her manager's outburst, she simultaneously demonstrated her own power and invalidated her boss's power over her. Perhaps the boss avoided future attacks for fear of losing more public face by Tammie's lack of reaction.

Shortly after the start of the Ukrainian War in 2022, Ukraine entered their first round of peace talks with Russia. The Ukrainians were unprepared for the former-KGB negotiation tactics their adversary employed. The Russians toyed with their emotions. They made personal attacks. They attempted to humiliate the Ukrainians during discussions. These attacks always came under the guise of being cooperative. It was a mental game. The goal was to prevent the Ukrainians from thinking straight. Luliia Osmolovska was an advisor to the Ukrainian government with experience in Russian negotiations. Luliia emphasized that Ukrainian negotiators must maintain a poker face if they are to hold their ground against the Russians during these talks.[9]

Daniel was a business manager working for a semiconductor company. He was clean-cut, clear-eyed, and came to work dressed in a suit and tie. He managed the company's largest customer. This customer provided nearly half a billion dollars in annual revenue for the company. Unfortunately, the customer ran into issues with Daniel's latest product.

Daniel made a visit to the customer's headquarters. The meeting took place in a large conference room. Daniel sat on one side of the table with his team. The team included his director and two of his direct reports. Across the table sat a gang of customer engineers. Both sides discussed the recent events. Daniel had no magic bullet to solve the issues quickly.

One engineer, clearly upset by the struggle, interrupted with a string of expletives aimed at Daniel himself. The scathing personal attack jolted the room into silence. The caustic words hung in the air.

Daniel was shocked. He turned to his director to see if she would defend him. The director sat with her mouth closed. She wasn't going to risk her neck by angering the customer further. He scanned the rest of the room. No one made eye contact with him.

Daniel's pulse raced. Should he defend himself? Should he say nothing? He took a long breath. Then another. Then he looked at the customer and said as calmly as he could, "I do not appreciate being called these words. If you would like to continue this conversation, please treat me with respect." His director's eyes widened. The engineer scowled. Then the engineer stood up and stormed out, slamming the door behind him.

After the engineer left, the meeting continued with the remaining staff. It turned out to be a productive meeting. As things wound down and everyone rose to leave, the angry engineer returned. The engineer walked up to Daniel, his demeanor calmer now. Then the engineer apologized for his behavior. The two shook hands.

Daniel focused on his boundary, not the attack. He acted, he did not react. That was Daniel's power. Had Daniel become defensive or attacked the client, it would have signaled a reaction and damaged the business relationship. Had Daniel become apologetic, it would have signaled another reaction. Reacting to bad behavior signals power loss. Instead, Daniel responded by setting clear boundaries on how he expected to be treated. Daniel showed self-respect and was respected for doing so. No doubt his display of power contributed to a mutually beneficial meeting outcome.

Joel Peterson, former chairman of JetBlue Airways, shared similar advice for successful negotiations. He said that when you encounter bad behavior in negotiations, it's important to remain calm.[10] Additionally, Joel recommended calling out bad behavior. He suggested that if someone starts yelling at you, you can respond calmly, "why are you yelling?" Take the high road, don't react. If this doesn't work, close your body language to them or walk away.

Boundaries demonstrate your mettle. Groups want their leaders to be strong. The practice of self-respect shows your capability not only to protect yourself but to protect the group. During startup pitches, I see investors frequently harangue entrepreneurs by voicing doubts. Investors call this "kicking the tires." They want to observe how entrepreneurs respond under pressure. It's a test to gauge the robustness of the startup's leadership. A leader needs to stay focused to appear powerful. If a leader gets defensive or folds under pressure, how can that leader be trusted to run the company? You must take responsibility for yourself if you want to be seen as capable of taking responsibility for others. If you can maintain your composure when someone has an outburst against you, those watching will see you as powerful and the outburst as weak, diminishing the outburst's effect.

But standing up for ourselves is hard because it plays right into our fear of rejection. Standing up not only feels threatening to our career, it threatens our desire to belong. And at work, the fear of not belonging is intensified by the illusion that the group controls our livelihood. When David Owens studied status behaviors in informal hierarchies (discussed in Chapter 5), he found that those with the lowest status focused on fitting in. Low-status members frequently ingratiated themselves through flattery. Low-status members also took on undervalued roles and menial tasks. They wanted to be liked. In David's own words, they "focused on the social and emotional aspects of group life."[11] Unfortunately, low-status behaviors only reinforce the dynamic of disempowerment.

One interesting area of power research suggests that if a manager likes you and you act weak, they will continue to like you. And if a manager dislikes you and you act weak, they will continue to dislike you.[12,13,14] Powerless behavior does not alter a situation, it merely reinforces the situation. Powerless behavior reinforces the perspective others already have. When someone treats you poorly and you seek their approval, you only confirm that they were right to treat you poorly. Reaction ratifies the action.

Pause for a moment to take in the last paragraph. When you act powerless, you have no influence on the environment. *Powerless behavior is powerless.* This means when someone attacks you and you react, you surrender your power in that situation. Like a son or daughter screaming at their overbearing parents, "don't treat me like a child!," those very words only reinforce the pattern of the existing relationship. Everyone watching will notice your lack of power.

We've all heard the term "nice guys finish last." This of course is not true. In an interview with Prince Harry of England and his wife Meghan Markle, Meghan said her only question before agreeing to meet Harry initially was, "[is] he nice? Because if he wasn't kind, it didn't seem like it would make sense."[15] Being nice to others is a great practice to live by. The issue isn't nice or not, the issue is weak or not.

When we try to win the approval of others, we react out of fear. Fear-based behavior includes defensiveness, automatic capitulation, and excessive apologizing, all of which signal low power.[*,14,16] People intuitively perceive such behavior as weak. Weak people have no influence.

---

*Apologizing is a healthy way to take accountability when you hurt someone or fail in your duty. Apologizing becomes weak when you apologize for your own self-expression. Apologizing for your boundaries, your needs, or your voice is self-negating.

We see self-negating behavior very clearly in romantic relationships. A man I knew in passing said his wife was losing attraction for him. She started blaming him for everything going wrong. Out of fear, he bent over backwards to make her happy. He stopped standing up for himself in order to display his commitment to her. When she argued, he capitulated. His motto was *don't rock the boat.* Because he didn't recognize the value he contributed to the relationship, he got locked in a cycle of chronic giving. His lack of self-respect created a massive power imbalance that made him even less attractive to his partner, destroying the mutual respect required for a healthy relationship. They ended up divorced. The message is there's nothing sexy in giving away your power to avoid conflict. It shows fear, it shows weakness, and it leaves you feeling even more hurt and embarrassed afterwards.

When someone blames you for events, it's their weakness. Blame is low-power behavior. And while responsibility is powerful, letting someone beat you down with blame is not. When someone blames you without acknowledging their contribution to the situation, respond with the facts. Almost all conflicts are jointly created, whether through action or inaction. Sometimes conflicts are created as a result of you withholding your boundaries. Own your part, and make others accountable for their part.

We all want to be close with others, to belong to groups. The big difference between the powerful and the powerless is that the powerful focus on their inner desire for connection, and the powerless focus on pleasing others out of fear. Don't ask yourself how you should act to be liked. Other people's happiness is not your number one priority. Instead, ask yourself what you want. The message here is that it's safe to focus on your goals, even though it doesn't always feel that way.

When I spoke to a city council member in a suburb outside Houston about her successful relationship with the local community, her motto was, "I'm here to help you. I don't care if you like me."[17] For me, treating others kindly gives me a warm feeling. It comes from the inside out, not the outside in. There is freedom there. Freedom is a much better reward than social validation.

Honor Your Resources

Anita is another corporate rockstar who faced a power threat. She was a director at a Fortune 500 tech company. She stood at a skinny 5'4". Other than her sharp eyes and previous work at Stanford, there was nothing about her that echoed power. She spent most of her time surrounded by men towering over her.

Sunlight poured into the staff conference room. Laptops sat open around the table. It was a typical California morning. The assembled directors reviewed tasks for an upcoming project. Anita was relatively new and carving out her place in the group. Everyone else in the room had worked at the company for years. They had a feel for each other. As the group proceeded through the agenda, up came a rudimentary task that needed attention. To a technology expert, it was busywork that amounted to the complexity of serving coffee. Without much forethought, one of the directors volunteered Anita.

Anita looked up, completely caught off-guard. Everyone stared at her with their usual polite corporate smiles. She blinked a few times like a deer caught in oncoming headlights. Then she leaned back. In a friendly but matter-of-fact way, Anita responded, "you hired me to work on our new process. This task is simple and time consuming. If this is the type of work you'd like me to do, perhaps it would be better if you hired some-one else." She gently closed her laptop and smiled politely right back at them.

There was a moment of silence as her words sank in. The corporate smiles vanished. Jaws dropped. Then at once everyone began apologizing. The woman who one moment ago faced relegation to menial task-doer vaulted herself gently into power. She respected her time and energy, and in doing so made it clear that she respected the value she brought to the table. After that, the group had a better feel for where Anita would stand in the status hierarchy.*

High-power individuals value their resources.[18] Our most important resources are our time and energy. The way we treat our resources shows self-respect. Legend tells the story of Alexander the Great invading India in the 4th century B.C.E. He learns of the Indian sage Dandamis living in the woods. Eager to speak with the sage, Alexander sends an advisor to fetch Dandamis. The advisor locates Dandamis and issues the proclamation, "Alexander, the Great son of Zeus, has ordered [you] to come to him. He will give you gold and other rewards but if you refuse, he may behead you."[19]

Dandamis listens to this idle threat. Then Dandamis replies that Alexander is no god, and to "go and tell your King that Dandamis, therefore, will not come to [him]. If he needs Dandamis, he must come to me." The advisor relays the message back to Alexander.

Alexander, the Conqueror, the Greatest of Men, went to visit Dandamis in the woods.

Privilege your resources when others make demands on you. A Google director shared his approach to expanding his internal corporate power. When executive management issues him new projects, he frequently responds by asking which of his current projects would they like to deprioritize in order for him to pull in resources for the new project? The implicit message is that he's already contributing greatly, and his resources

---

*When we say "no" to something we don't want to do, we feel more positive emotions such as happiness, pride, and control. And when we say "yes" to something we don't want to do, we feel more negative emotions such as regret, frustration, and stress. If you fail to stand up for yourself, not only do you appear less powerful on the outside, you feel worse on the inside.[25]

are finite. Executive management frequently responds by giving him additional resources such as headcount and budget to take on the new responsibility. These new resources expand the director's formal power. His approach is far more effective than those who silently accept everything piled on their plate until they're overloaded and underperforming.

Over the Christmas holidays, I arranged to meet with the CEO of a large organization. We set a time to talk at 4:30pm. I'm on the Zoom call five minutes early. He shows up five minutes late. Not unexpected. He shares his thoughts on power. I'm taking notes. We're both engaged. As the clock ticks toward the end of our meeting, I ask if he has a few extra minutes to spare. He pauses. Then he says he has five extra minutes. We talk exactly five extra minutes and say our goodbyes. It was a fantastic discussion. But what caught my attention most was the CEO's focus on time. I knew he had no pressing matters forcing him off the call over the holidays, he was simply placing a boundary.

When someone asks you when you're free to meet, do you find yourself saying "anytime?" If you're too available, perhaps it shows that you don't value your time because you give it away so freely. Or perhaps it shows that your time isn't worth much since no one is consuming it. Just because you're available doesn't mean others have a right to your time. Your schedule is one of your most powerful assertions of personal boundaries because your time represents your commitment to your goals and your life. Your schedule can be a list of intentional actions versus reactions. When you arrange to meet with someone, consider offering a few specific options rather than giving them a blank check to meet "anytime."

There are many other ways to protect your time. CEOs often respond with very short emails.[20] They don't waste time on fluff. Likewise, when you stick to a meeting agenda and don't allow others to stray off-topic, it signals you respect your time as well as everyone else's. I know a very successful startup founder who has a unique approach to investor meetings. At the start of a meeting, he tells investors that if they don't believe in his business idea after his opening pitch, he's not interested in going through the empty motions of Q&A discussion. Everyone wins with this approach. When you respect your resources, others respect you.

How to Say No

Let's put you to the test. Your client asks you to stay late working with them on a project. It's an important client and an important project. But it's Wednesday evening, your weekly scheduled date night with your partner. You might choose to complete the work, in which case you'll have to say no to your partner. Or you might decide the higher value here is your relationship. Let's assume you choose your partner and reject your client's request. The fact that you hold your boundary is an assertion of your personal power. But what words do you use to say no? A typical response to the client might be, "I can't work late on Wednesdays. I have date night with my partner." Ouch. With these words you could get hurt.

Vanessa Patrick explored the most powerful way to say "no" when upholding a boundary.[21] She recruited participants to imagine offering chocolate cake to guests at a party. Guests either refused the offer, saying "I *can't* eat chocolate cake," or saying "I *don't* eat chocolate cake." The only difference was the use of a single word, *can't* or *don't*.

The word shift between *can't* and *don't* conveys a huge mindset difference. According to the research, *can't* implies a deference to external pressures, whereas *don't* is grounded in one's identity. The result? When guests rejected the offer with the words "I don't," participants saw guests as more persuasive, having more conviction, and more rooted in their own identity than those who said "I can't."

Vanessa concluded that using the words "I don't" is a form of empowered refusal. She said, "empowered refusal is a way of saying no that effectively conveys your stance based on your values, preferences, and priorities."[22] When you demonstrate internal drive, you convey personal power. Equally important, Vanessa's research suggests that empowered refusal is less likely to receive push-back.

Of course, you can always dodge the bullet by saying "I can't" and blaming your behavior on outside forces. But dodging the bullet comes at the cost of losing your power in the eyes of others. Your weak rejection is more likely to receive push-back. And if you dodge the bullet to feel safe, know that seeking safety reinforces your low-power psychology.

Vanessa ran another experiment to test empowered refusal in which participants tried to sell a local newspaper subscription to prospective customers. Each participant launched into their sales pitch. All the prospects, who were undercover research assistants, rejected the sales pitches in one of two ways. Some prospects said, "I *can't* spend money without checking my budget first." Other prospects said, "I *don't* spend money without checking my budget first." Results showed that prospects who rejected the offer with the words "I don't" were again seen as more persuasive and having more conviction by the participants.*

Back to your client asking you to work late on date night. What do you say now?

Voice Your Needs

Tom was hired out of college into a Fortune 100 company. With his PhD in Aeronautics, he was a strong fit for the company's aircraft design branch. The company had just gone through a

---

*Consider other language shifts that root your behavior internally rather than externally. For example, you can replace "should" with "could." You can also replace "I have to" with "I choose to."

merger. As part of the restructure, the company collapsed their 12-point seniority scale into six levels. Tom was one of their first new hires after the restructure. Tom's PhD experience put him at a level 7 on the old seniority scale, right between levels 3 and 4 on the new scale. With a promise and a handshake, the company brought him in at a level 3 and said they'd make an instant effort to start the process of becoming a level 4.

Four years later, Tom was still a level 3.

Frustrated, Tom accepted an offer at another company. He handed in his resignation to his employer. What Tom did not know was that his employer recently signed a multi-million-dollar contract with a client that depended on his skills. There were a lot of people counting on Tom, and no time to train someone new.

The moment Tom handed in his resignation, the power dynamic shifted. The company scrambled. They asked Tom what he wanted. Part of him simply wanted to leave. But he had roots in the company. He told the company to fulfill the promise they made him four years ago. He asked for a promotion to level 4. He got it. He asked that his compensation match the offer from the other company, a 20% bump in salary. They matched it.

Tom stayed.

The company didn't keep Tom down for four years out of malice. They simply overlooked his needs. The relationship had fallen into the traditional roles of employer and employee, boss and workhorse. The company went along with the expectation that Tom would do the job. After all, why wouldn't he? What Tom didn't realize was how much power he had. Tom had the skills, and the company needed those skills to run the business. When Tom handed in his resignation, his needs became visible again.

Relationships between two parties evolve over time. As they evolve, you need to assess whether the relationship remains fair. No one is looking out for you, it's up to you to look out for yourself. Sometimes it feels like a dance between being happy and resentful. When you begin to feel resentful, you may want to reassess what you're receiving. Your compensation is not your manager's responsibility. In Tom's case, he took the nuclear option and resigned. But Tom confided that he could have spoken to his manager sooner rather than let his resentment build up.

People may give you less than you deserve. They may abuse you. They may put undue burden on your time. If you allow this disrespect to persist, it eats you up on the inside and often broadcasts your lack of power to the outside. People don't respect victims, they respect strength.

We all desire approval at some level, but we cannot truly get it without first honoring ourselves. Self-respect means speaking up boldly for our worth and boldly for our boundaries. Speaking up requires courage because it requires us to face the fear of rejection. We may briefly anger others when we ask for fair compensation or hold a boundary. But other people's feelings are not our primary concern, our goals are. And the respect we earn by standing up for ourselves will make those relationships stronger. When we stop asking whether we are good enough for others and start asking ourselves whether the situation serves us, that's when we begin to step into our power.

Now it's time to explore the source of strong boundaries.

The Power of Forgiveness

No one escapes being hurt or attacked in life. When others treat us poorly, we demand justice. Those who cannot find justice wallow in resentment. Research suggests the desire for revenge is associated with low power, not high. When we are powerful, we feel more positive and we move forward with our lives rather than wallow in resentment. For these reasons, personal power is tied to forgiveness.

There are many reasons power is associated with forgiveness, including the fact that forgiveness restores a sense of control. But one of the most important reasons that power leads to forgiveness is that power restores a sense of justice. When we forgive someone, we reestablish consensus that a value was violated. After all, you can't forgive someone if they did nothing wrong. Forgiveness therefore reaffirms the value's importance. We also put ourselves in the morally powerful position by affirming we hold an important value that the other person has violated.[26,27]

If you were the victim of bad behavior, one way to restore your power in that relationship is to express your forgiveness. Think about what you will say and how you will forgive the violator. Then find a medium to express your forgiveness. You might have a conversation with the violator or you might email them. It's up to you. Perhaps you are most comfortable writing your forgiveness down on a sheet of paper and keeping that to yourself rather than sending it off.

Do not expect an apology or a particular response from the violator. Expecting something from another person only gives away your power. Forgiveness seeks nothing because forgiveness is personal expression.

Personal power comes from rooting internally. Personal power comes from action. Personal power comes from moving forward. And personal power comes from self-expression. Let the act of forgiveness be a gateway back to your power.

7 | Find Your Bedrock

Sonar was *the* unicorn startup of Silicon Valley. The app provided a unique way to meet people using social media connections. When someone was nearby with similar interests, Sonar buzzed in your pocket. It became one of the hottest apps to hit the market in 2011. Millions of people downloaded it. Everyone wanted a piece of the company.

Sonar raised $2 million in investment. The founders were invited to speak at prestigious events. They were featured in all the major news outlets from *The New York Times* and CNN to CNBC and *TIME*. Until they weren't.

The company folded in 2013.

Shocked enthusiasts questioned how this could happen. Founder Brett Martin wrote a post-mortem on the failure.[1] He shared that as the app's popularity grew, customers began proposing new product ideas. Meanwhile, the competition pumped out new features. Brett found himself altering Sonar's roadmap to build what others were building. He lost focus on his own goals out of fear of being left behind. And Sonar went from being a leader to a follower.

This chapter focuses on self-direction. Powerful people are ideologically driven. Rather than let the world define them, these individuals manifest their interests into the world. They stand for something in the face of adversity. Their ability to take a stand is what provides the backbone to their boundaries and attracts others to them. But how does self-direction show up in powerful people?

Anchor In

During a warm summer evening in Washington D.C., a group of friends came together for a backyard party. There was a sense of merriment in the air as the group chatted over wine and cheese. The hours passed by affectionately as sunset faded into night. The crickets began chirping. The stars twinkled.

Abruptly a gun flashed into view. The gun was held point-blank at the head of one of the women. "Give me your money or I'm gonna start shooting!" Everyone froze. The gun was wielded by a stranger in a sweatsuit who emerged from the shadows.[2]

A moment passed as everyone remained frozen. Then the party guests checked their pockets and purses. No one had cash. The stranger kept shouting for money and threatening to shoot! Unable to comply, some of the guests lashed back in anger, reproaching the stranger like parents scolding a child. This only made the stranger more agitated as he continued to shout. The moment looked grim.

Then from the backyard table, one friend offered kindly, "We're here celebrating. Why don't you have a glass of wine and sit down?"

And a funny thing happened. The look on the stranger's face softened. The energy of the moment shifted. The stranger took a glass, had a sip. "That's a really good glass of wine," he said. Then he tucked the gun away and sat down at the table.

The friends plus one spoke together over wine and cheese for a while. After some time, the stranger said quietly, "I think I've come to the wrong place." He stood up, apologized, asked for a few hugs, and left.

Despite the obvious trauma that left everyone a bit shaken, the group of friends felt a sense of wonderment for what had just occurred.

So what's going on here? Before we answer, let's switch gears.

Imagine you created a new pasta, never before seen or tasted by humankind. You're about to become a living legend with your product. But before it goes to market, it needs a name. Something creative. There is a pantheon of pastas out there with names like lasagna, ravioli, rigatoni, linguini, and spaghetti. What name do you choose for your new noodle?

Come up with a name right now and say it aloud. Make this exercise real.

Got a name? Good.

Adam Galinsky and his colleagues ran a similar experiment asking students to come up with names for new products like pasta and painkillers.[3] Before asking students to name these products, Adam primed half the students to feel high power. The other half were left unprimed to act as normal. After students named the products, Adam assessed how creative the names were. What signified creativity? In this case, creativity meant choosing a pasta name that did not end in a familiar sound like na, li, ni, or ti. Yup, it had to be completely different from the examples listed.

High-power people were significantly more creative in their product naming than the average person. Similar experiments asked powerful people to come up with new menu items at restaurants or imagine what aliens look like. And in each case, personal power fostered the most creative examples. Creativity is associated with big-picture thinking. But perhaps more importantly, creativity is associated with independence over conformity. Powerful people tuned out external stimuli in order to listen to what arose from within. They anchored internally.

The source of creativity may appear unrelated to the events of a gunman and a glass of wine, but tuning out the external noise and anchoring inward is exactly what happened in the backyard that night.

When someone takes an action, be it a friend or a foe, they influence those around them. Love is met with love. Anger is met with anger. We see this at the conscious level, but the same process is happening unconsciously as well.[4] For example, if someone believes you are a loving person, they will unconsciously act in ways that cause you to automatically respond more lovingly. Or if someone believes you are incompetent, they will treat you in ways that influence you to act more incompetently. And it's all happening beneath our awareness. Psychologists call this *behavioral confirmation*, in which one person's expectation of others causes others to respond in ways that confirm the expectation. Research out of the University of Kentucky showed exactly that – when two people worked on a task together, the negative expectations of the more powerful person influenced their partner to act more consistent with those expectations, even when the other person knew nothing about those expectations.[5] It's a self-fulfilling prophecy driven by the person with more power. And the more power someone has in a situation, the more likely their expectations will influence the behavior of those around them. Personal power is the key to the whole automatic roleplay.*

Now if a gun-wielding stranger sees others as enemies, his dominant behavior disempowers others and causes them to react in ways that meet his expectations. Regardless of whether others comply or fight back, others' low-power reactions merely confirm the expectations of the powerful. But something was different that warm summer night. When one of the

---

*Behavioral confirmation is one of the insidious drivers that reinforce stereotyping and discrimination. The unconscious stereotype expectations of one person may lead those being stereotyped to unconsciously respond in ways that appear to confirm the stereotype, resulting in discrimination.[27] It's a terrible trap brought about by those with the power to enforce their views onto those who experience less power.

guests offered the stranger a glass of wine instead of reacting to his threat, she conveyed her own power to enforce a new narrative of friendship. Suddenly the stranger, who was likely living in a world of internal disempowerment and pain despite his dominant behavior, couldn't help but react positively to this gesture of warmth.

"The world will ask you who you are. And if you don't know, the world will tell you," said Carl Jung. When we are not anchored in our thoughts and values, we absorb the messages and values of those around us. We react to the behaviors of others in ways that fulfill their expectations of us rather than demonstrate our own capabilities, just as we might name a pasta the way others before us have.

Instinctively, we may anchor externally for security. Many of us chase social achievements in order to be admired – whether it's a great job, money, or a social media following. The lure of these goals is almost intoxicating because it speaks to our need for acceptance. But when our goal is admiration, we've turned our attention outward seeking approval. We're following the siren call of other people's evaluations.

The grandfather of the self-esteem movement, Nathaniel Branden, shared the following words on seeking approval: "Within you is a void that should have been filled by self-esteem. When you attempt to fill it with the approval of others instead, the void grows deeper and the hunger for acceptance and approval grows stronger."[6] No amount of external admiration can bring about a robust experience of personal power. Even in the victory of approval there is defeat. The first destructive consequence of looking outward is that we lose inward focus. Without a clear inner anchor, next we lose our boundaries. We may turn to distractions and reactions. Soon we find ourselves drifting endlessly toward whatever is handed to us in the hopes that something we are given will bring us enduring joy. Nothing ever does.

Personal power is not about being productive, wealthy, or exercising every day. Power is about where we put our anchor. One of the strongest qualities of personal power is that power makes us trust ourselves more.[7] We look inward for our North Star to guide us. As we tune into our feelings and beliefs, we tune out the involuntary influence of others. This might be as simple as pausing to take a breath before making a decision. The result is that power makes us less influenced by persuasion and more judicious of the advice we receive. While we may go wrong occasionally, *personal power is not about being wrong or right, it's about anchoring internally.* After failure, the powerful are more likely to reflect on their actions and learn from them.[8] Learning continues to build self-trust. Whereas the powerless, having surrendered their thinking to the outside world, more often blame their failure on others. There is nothing so powerless as saying, "it was his fault," or "she made me do it."[*] In this way, powerlessness never builds self-trust because there is no acknowledgment of personal responsibility.[**]

How We See Ourselves

Personal power impacts how we evaluate ourselves. One of the greatest benefits of power is that it raises our self-esteem and self-confidence. Naturally the more we trust ourselves, the more confident we feel. Conversely, those with low power are more self-conscious, concerned with how others view them rather than their own perspective.[9]

But one fascinating study conducted by Pablo Briñol showed that power can also hamper self-confidence.[10] Pablo

---

[*]We also disempower ourselves when we make others responsible for our feelings. For example, it is common to say, "he made me angry." When we attribute our feelings to others, we obstruct the development of healthy emotional intelligence.

[**]The sad flip side is that the powerless may attribute their accomplishments externally as well, leading to imposter syndrome.

took students and instructed half of them to sit in a high-power pose with a straight back, and the other half to sit curled over in a low-power position. He then instructed students in each group to list either three positive traits or three negative traits about their professional readiness for work. In total there were four subgroups: high-power writing positive things about themselves, high-power writing negative things about themselves, low-power writing positive things about themselves, and low-power writing negative things about themselves. Afterward, Pablo measured whether each student believed they would make a good employee on the job market.

I love this study because it shows something completely unexpected. First, for the low-power students, regardless of whether they wrote down positive or negative traits about themselves, personal reflection did not impact how they felt about their own capability to work. Because low-power students discounted their own thoughts, self-reflection was irrelevant to them.*

There is a famous quote attributed to Henry Ford, "If you think you can or you think you can't – you're right." This quote fits alongside a new age concept called manifestation, that if you imagine something, then it will come to you. But evidence suggests these beliefs are simply not true if you are not in your power. With low power, whether you think you can or not, it doesn't matter.** To foster self-esteem and manifest a new reality for yourself, your very first step has to be stepping out of powerlessness.

---

*Research out of Indiana University suggests that when low-power individuals behave in ways that meet the expectations of the powerful, low-power individuals begin to believe that their expectation-driven behavior is who they actually are.[28] They lose sight of their true selves.

**Consider this effect as nature's protection mechanism. When you are filled with fear and anxiety and most prone to negative thinking, you are least likely to manifest what you think – a safeguard against those negative thoughts. On the flip side, you are more vulnerable to the energy of the environment around you.

High-power students showed completely different results. When high-power students wrote down positive traits about themselves, they felt more capable to enter the workforce. And when high-power students wrote down negative traits, they felt less capable. The powerful students who wrote down negative traits about themselves even believed they were less capable to work than the low-power students!

What Pablo's research showed is that powerful people believe in their thoughts, whether good or bad. While powerful people generally hold higher regard for themselves by default, if pressed to reflect on their weaknesses, they will feel more negatively.[11]

This brings us to the main point. To tap into your power, it's crucial you tune into what you know and believe. You cannot continually doubt your thoughts and suppress your feelings and still experience a deep enduring sense of power.* And having tuned into yourself, it becomes important to focus on your positive traits to reinforce your feelings of capability.

How We See Others

"Why should we listen to you?"

Becky was greeted with these words when she stepped into the IMD lecture hall. IMD is the ivory tower of European business academics. The university regularly ranks as the top business school in the world. Notable alumni include former Nestlé CEO Paul Bulcke, Netherlands Prime Minister Mark Rutte, and Indian billionaire Tarang Jain.

Becky was fresh off the plane, having just arrived on the IMD campus after securing a faculty role there. Her eyes exuded a

---

*When you are aware of your feelings, even when you feel fear or anxiety, you begin to tap into your personal power because you anchor inwards. Conversely, disconnecting from your feelings or blindly reacting to your feelings signifies an absence of personal power.

deep intellect under a pair of black-rimmed glasses. She recently completed her PhD on interpersonal dynamics. Her research landed her the coveted position at IMD. It was her first day on the job, and her students took no time holding her to the fire.

"Why should we listen to you?" one of them challenged.

Fun way to begin your first day at work. How would you respond if you were in Becky's shoes?

The worst response would be to take the challenge personally. Defensiveness acknowledges the other person's power over us. But there is a second common response that is almost equally damaging. Imagine a 1960s movie scene. The place is Moscow. The main character is apprehended by the KGB. She finds herself in an interrogation room completely dark save for a lone lamp. On one side of the table sits a shadowy KGB agent. On the other side sits our unlucky character. The lamp shines its blinding light at one of the two people sitting there. Can you guess who? The light illustrates the dynamic of power. It is always the one with less power who is under the light of evaluation.[12]

As Becky entered the lecture hall, the evaluation lamp cast its glow on her. The normal response would be for Becky to state her credentials. After all, she was an academic star in her own right. But any such response would instantly validate the student's power to evaluate her, putting her in the weaker position. Not the best way to build a reputation your first day on the job. She could ignore the comment. Another option for sure.

Becky was no spring chicken to this game of power. She had devoted the last four years of her thesis research to studying interpersonal dynamics. Becky turned to the student. Paused. Then said, "I don't really care whether you listen to me. I'm much more concerned with what I think of you."

Check and mate. Becky had the students eating out of the palm of her hand afterward.

Self-direction shows up when you evaluate a situation. Anchored in your perspective, you shine your attention outward like a spotlight seeking information in pursuit of your goals. When you seek information, you evaluate others with respect to your goals. Evaluation is the essence of high-power awareness. When you evaluate, you communicate that you are internally driven.

Years ago I attended a personal growth seminar with several hundred attendees. The entrance price was a modest $1,000. Toward the end of the event, the host delivered his upsell. Attendees could join a small exclusive community with him for the price of $30,000. Quite the upsell. The host gave a few benefits to joining the community. Then he placed a restriction. He would only accept 10 people into the program. Salespeople use scarcity tactics like this all the time to make their offer seem more valuable. Limited space creates demand. But the host wasn't finished. He said that to be one of those special 10, you had to go through an interview selection process. In other words, he would evaluate whether you were worthy of being in his $30,000 program. A genius power move. Suddenly I was listening.

This example illustrates the power of evaluation. Many in the audience including myself had the knee-jerk reaction to ask ourselves whether we were worthy. I wanted to go through the interview process simply to know whether I was good enough. This totally distracted me from evaluating whether I actually wanted the product. Typically it is the seller who is selling and the buyer who is evaluating. By spinning the attention away from justifying the price tag to forcing the audience to justify they were worthy of the program, he reversed the power dynamic. The seller became the buyer and the buyer became the seller. The host shined the spotlight at the audience. And by placing himself in the powerful position, the host made his program more desirable.

Shining attention outward is the same spotlight principle found in Chapter 5. There, the spotlight is shined on different team members to elicit their input. But whereas being in the spotlight and sharing ideas can heighten one's power, being under evaluation lowers it. Thus, being in the spotlight is not a consistent way to show up big. Being in the spotlight is not the source of power, power comes from being in control of the spotlight.

Rod is a networking guru in the North American technology scene. He is well-connected and attends lavish parties where dancers pour champagne into glasses from tightropes crisscrossing the ceiling. That kind of guy. Rod utilizes his network to recruit speakers, usually wealthy magnates, to his innovation conference. When Rod flew to Washington to recruit a corporate executive as his conference keynote speaker, he found himself in a spacious office. The exec sat behind a massive mahogany desk. As Rod entered, the exec waved Rod to sit down and then spent the next few minutes wrapping up emails and making Rod wait. The meeting was clearly going to be on the exec's timeline. Finally the exec turned to Rod and asked a simple question, why should the exec take time from his busy schedule to speak at Rod's conference?

Rod thought about it for a moment. Then he responded, "Let's not move too fast. I'd like to find out first whether you'd be a good fit for the conference." The conversation progressed from there. The meeting turned out to be mutually engaging. By the end, the exec was interested. But Rod decided later to invite a billionaire to do the keynote. That kind of guy.

Behind powerful evaluation is curiosity. Curiosity focuses on learning. High-power people are ultimately learners in service to their goals.[13] Learning can include learning about the environment or evaluating whether someone will be a good fit for their team. When done right, learning comes off as interest and not arrogance, listening and not judgment. True learning is to be "in a position to agree or to disagree with an idea."[14]

Learning displays openness to new ideas, and openness corre-
lates with personal power.[15] Curiosity and learning arise from
your internal anchors. You are not there to dominate others, you
are there to stand in your own power. When you are in a high-
pressure situation, you can remind yourself not to react, appease,
nor judge. Instead, stay curious.

Captains and Players

Cristian is a sales executive who wears a wide smile and treats
his employees to sushi during afternoon meetings. He's the type
of manager who would rather drive his employees home in his
Mercedes than make them take public transit. Cristian is equally
generous with customers. He frequently visits companies to
build relationships and drum up new business.

One potential customer he visited was the manager of a
small factory producing automobile parts. Cristian sat down
with the manager and exchanged a few pleasantries. Then the
manager leaned back and said he was ready to hear Cristian's
pitch. Cristian became silent for a moment, tapping his finger
on his knee. Then Cristian said that he didn't believe his business
was the right fit for the manager's factory.

And . . . Full stop. Say what?

Cristian's response is not what normally happens when
a salesperson walks into the room. The standard script is that
the salesperson pitches a product and the customer evaluates
and voices hesitations. The factory manager had no idea how
to respond to this new script. After a moment, the manager
began explaining why his factory would make a solid partnership for Cristian. The conversation progressed with the manager
attempting to sell the partnership and Cristian voicing hesitation. The power dynamic had reversed.

To understand what happened here, let's turn to an experiment run by John Copeland.[16] John invited participants into

his office to play a team game. Do you remember playing team games on the school playground? First the group selects team captains. Then the captains take turns choosing players until everyone is on one team or the other. When participants arrived in John's office, John assigned each of them to be either a captain or a player. Captains chose players for their teams. But there was a catch – too many players showed up. All players wanted to play for the cash prizes involved, but there was not enough space for everyone to join a team. John said it was up to the captains to choose the best players.

Team selection provided an excellent backdrop for John to observe power dynamics. The captains had all the power to choose, and the players were at the captain's mercy. Based on the instructions, each captain first met with one player. For 10 minutes, the captain and the player spoke. Then the experiment ended. That was it. There was no actual game. All John wanted to find out was how the captain and the player interacted during the selection process.

John's experiment shed light on the behaviors of this power dynamic. Captains evaluated players to determine if players could help achieve the goal of winning the game. Evaluation is high-power behavior. But equally interesting was how players responded. Players focused on proving that they were good at the game so they would be chosen. Proving is low-power behavior.

Proving is the opposite side of evaluation. Proving is a form of approval-seeking that puts us into the weak position. Proving (or justifying yourself) inherently seeks validation, thereby ratifying the other person's power to bestow it to us. When we attempt to prove ourselves, we also convey other subtle signs that diminish our power. For example, proving language instinctively focuses on concrete details of competence over an abstract focus on the big picture.[17] You could be using all the persuasion in the world to convince someone to accept you. But if the frame of your discussion is saturated with this power imbalance, it dulls the effect of all your persuasive efforts.*

When the factory manager began proving to Cristian why his company would make a great customer, the factory manager temporarily took a lower position of power. This position reflected more power toward Cristian. And the more power Cristian secured in the dynamic, the more valuable he appeared to the manager. Cristian respected the manager, so he did not employ this strategy as a form of manipulation. Cristian genuinely believed his business wasn't a good fit. His power came from honoring and verbalizing his perspective. In the end and despite the manager's most adamant arguments, which became even more adamant the more Cristian demurred, Cristian chose not to partner together. It really wasn't the best fit.

Set Your Goal

Proving frequently shows up when you enter high-stakes situations like customer meetings or job interviews. For example, when you step into an interview, you expect to answer the employer's questions. But have you ever wondered why it's equally important to ask questions during an interview? No doubt asking questions shows your interest in the job. But if interest were the only reason asking questions was important, then showing excitement should be sufficient, and it isn't. Some people say that asking questions helps you gauge whether you'll enjoy the role. But if asking questions only serves you, then why should asking questions have any impact on whether you are hired or not?

---

*Proving also shows up when we defend ourselves against accusations. If we are innocent and persist in proving our innocence, we weaken the very argument we attempt to make. This is one of the genius reasons a justice system based on "innocent until proven guilty" is necessary for the fair protection of all citizens within a society.

Sonia Kang paired business students together to run a job negotiation exercise.[18] She assigned one student to be the recruiter and the other to be the job candidate. When Sonia told students the negotiation was only a class exercise, the students felt almost no pressure to perform. But when Sonia told students that the exercise was a real evaluation of the students' negotiation abilities, students in the traditionally low-power role of job candidate performed far worse. These students literally choked under the pressure of trying to prove themselves.

When you walk into a situation with the intent to prove yourself, you create a huge amount of stress because you want to succeed but feel a low sense of control over the outcome. In the case of an interview, you anchor your self-worth in the judgment of the interviewer. As a result of this stress, your ability to think clearly deteriorates and your performance plummets.[18]

Sonia found an easy way to counteract the detrimental effects of evaluation stress – job candidates spent roughly five minutes reflecting on the meaning and relevance of their personal values before the negotiation. In other words, job candidates anchored internally. Anchoring internally eliminated the need to prove themselves. When candidates entered the negotiation after reflecting on their values, they did fine.* In fact, these candidates were nearly twice as likely to make the first offer in salary discussions, a typical high-power behavior.

When you enter an interview with a focus on answering questions but not asking, you're likely focused on proving yourself. You also grant the interviewer the entire power of agenda. These behaviors solidify your low power in the exchange and diminish your perceived value.

You can reduce your feelings of pressure and improve your performance by entering interviews with a clear goal to

---

*Research suggests that reflecting on personal values prior to performance reduces the gender achievement gap by 40%.[29]

determine whether the job will be a good fit for you. HR representatives say that the purpose of a job interview is to determine whether a candidate is a good fit for the position.[19] This is an objective goal. Specifying goals like this is shown to improve outcomes in negotiations.[20] When you step into an interview with an objective goal such as determining whether the job will be a good fit for you, you anchor in your power.

Focused on your goal, you will naturally ask questions during the interview to seek information. Asking questions balances out the power dynamic. And the more power you show, the more your perceived value increases and you come across as a strong candidate. When the energy of an interview naturally switches from them evaluating you to them selling themselves, you know they're interested. I also find that one of the best signs of success in these high-stakes situations is not knowing how you did afterward. When you're completely engaged in the discussion and not focused on making a good impression, you're doing the meeting right.*

Elizabeth Nieto, the Global Chief Diversity and Inclusion Officer at MetLife, spoke on her success finding a fulfilling career. Elizabeth said, "I have been lucky enough in the last two jobs [that] part of my interview process [was] to interview with the CEO. And the same way that they were assessing me on my capabilities to do the job, I was assessing them on the commitment to the diversity and inclusion."[21]

The same rules apply to entrepreneurs raising money. Many of my startup clients tell me they feel intimidated when pitching to investors. Often these clients walk into investor meetings with the intent to prove that their startup is amazing, which backfires completely. Entrepreneurs who aim to prove not only

---

*Another useful way to shift your mindset is to recognize that this moment isn't about you, it's about service to your audience. When you focus on service, you step out of self-consciousness and into goal-focus.

create more anxiety for themselves, they send unconscious signals to investors that they are not powerful leaders. My clients do significantly better when they walk into investor meetings with a clear goal focus, such as identifying the best investor to join their board.

Your experience of low power during high-stakes meetings is not based on an objective view of reality, it's based on your focus. There's no reason to assume investors have all the power. They're desperate for the next big deal. And money is the most ubiquitous resource on the planet, whereas your experience and vision make you unique. Likewise, there's no reason to assume in job interviews that the interviewer has all the power. If companies had all the power, they would not spend billions of dollars annually trying to recruit the best candidates.

You can change your focus during high stakes meeting to be in service to your goals, and that will change your experience of personal power.

Stay the Course

The 1980s were characterized by violence as Apartheid entered its death throes. South African politicians spoke against racism publicly but made little effort behind closed doors to change. South African police continued to gun down Black citizens in the streets. Armed White vigilante groups targeted Black progressive leaders. The Black population lashed back in violence against oppression. There would be at least five reported massacres in South Africa that decade. The country was tearing itself apart.

Amid the chaos, Nelson Mandela remained imprisoned. From behind bars, he gained popularity for his steady rhetoric supporting democracy. In 1985, Prime Minister Pieter Botha invited Mandela to denounce the Black violence in exchange for release. Mandela's daughter delivered his words to the public.

Rather than accept Botha's offer, Mandela stated that the violence would cease when there was real democracy. The masses cheered, but Mandela remained imprisoned.

Five long years later, Mandela was finally released. Shortly thereafter, he visited New York to speak at a town hall event. The scathing questions he received were anything but gentle. How does one of history's greatest leaders confront opposition?

First among these questions was Mandela's stance on racism in New York. The implication of the question was that if Mandela believed in racial equality, he ought to support equal rights in the United States as well. Mandela responded that he was in New York to gain support against Apartheid, not to judge the U.S. government. He condemned racism universally but believed the United States could handle their own internal affairs.

Then Mandela was challenged as to how he could accept the support of human rights violators like Colonel Qaddafi of Libya and Fidel Castro of Cuba. Mandela responded that just because the United States saw these people as evil did not mean that they could not be allies of South Africa. To many listeners, it sounded like Mandela ignored the iniquities of his allies so long as he received support from them. Feeling exactly this, Henry Sigmund stood up.

Sigmund was the executive director of the American Jewish Congress and a representative of Jewish organizations supporting Mandela's cause. Sigmund said he felt profound disappointment because Mandela's answer about Qaddafi and Castro suggested an amorality that ignored the list of human rights violations occurring in Libya and Cuba. Sigmund asked Mandela to clarify.

How would Mandela respond to the criticism of one of his greatest allies?

Mandela: *We are a liberation movement which is fully involved in a struggle to emancipate our people from one of the worst racial tyrannies the world has seen. We have no time to be looking into the internal affairs of other countries . . . I have been asked by somebody who wants me to express an opinion on the differences that are taking place within the USA . . . I have refused to be drawn into that. Why should Mr. Sigmund accept my refusal to be drawn into the internal affairs of the United States and at the same time want me to be involved in the internal affairs of Libya and Cuba? I refuse to do that . . . We are not prepared to be swayed by anybody. We have an independent policy which we assert no matter with whom we discuss.*[22]

Our heroes are not those who bend to the situation, our heroes are those who do not bend. From Mandela's pro-democracy message in 1985 to his town hall responses in New York, Mandela spoke straight. To Sigmund, Mandela's behavior appeared to conflict with Jewish causes. But in fact, Colonel Qaddafi once threatened that if Mandela employed Jews, he would not be allowed to maintain offices in Libya. Mandela stated that he would rather employ Jews than remain in Libya. Mandela took no sides but the side he stood for. He was consistent to his mission regardless of the external circumstance.

To feel powerful, we must anchor in our goals and values like Mandela. Values are the internal bedrock that give us a steady grip to adhere to. Values are rooted in the power of abstract thinking and give rise to visions. And when we communicate our values consistently, we win trust.[23]

Many politicians prevaricate on their values to stay in the good graces of their allies and constituents. As a result, political trust has been on the decline for decades. When a politician acts like a chameleon, showing no commitment to goals and values, how can they be trusted? These politicians lack an understanding of being diplomatically agile while being uncompromising on what's important, and they suffer for it. Externally, the apex of power these minor politicians seek remains forever beyond their grip precisely because they are unwilling to commit to their own values. And internally, these politicians undermine their own experience of personal power.

Researchers found that powerful people are significantly better at self-regulation, meaning they remain focused on their goals and values even in the face of temptation and exhaustion.[24] Acts of self-regulation that display personal power can range from prioritizing important long-term goals over short-term ones, as Mandela did, to something as simple as rejecting dessert when one has professed a desire to eat healthy. Mandela vividly displayed his power by remaining fixed on his goals despite the various bribes and threats from those around him. And when others witness a person show self-regulation by remaining fixed on their goals, they view that person as more powerful and are more willing to elect that person as a leader.[25,*] In sum, the powerful remain steadfastly focused on their goal pursuits, and others who witness this focus confer to them more power.

It's entirely likely that if Mandela had compromised on his pro-democracy vision in order to be released from jail in 1985, he would have lost public support. And with the loss of public support, the government might have lost motivation to release Mandela despite their agreement. It wasn't Mandela's comprise that led to his eventual release, it was his lack of compromise that swept him into power. As Winston Churchill once said, "You have enemies? Good. That means you've stood up for something, sometime in your life."[**]

---

*Observers who witness self-regulation in pursuit of goals also view the self-regulator as more assertive, competent, moral, and authentic.

**Churchill displayed similar traits to Mandela throughout his political career. Even in the disastrous campaign of Gallipoli during World War 1, Churchill supported that campaign to the bitter end.[30] And while Churchill got knocked down politically as a result of Gallipoli's failure (similar to Mandela's sustained incarceration), he rose back to become one of the 20th century's greatest leaders, just like Mandela. I have witnessed this phoenix fall and rise in many of history's greatest leaders so much so that I now wonder whether great leaders must go through such a test as a precondition to achieving greatness.

When to Walk Away

Up to now we've focused on the use of personal power in business, but power is universal in human relationships. To give you a sense of this, let's conclude with a high-stakes situation we might experience outside the office.

Linda's goal was marriage. The mother of two beautiful children from a whirlwind nuptial in her youth, she had been divorced the last 15 years. "I'm never getting married again," she once declared. Her life of serial monogamy suited her just fine. She owned a house near the beach and sported the latest fashion. She also had an endearing personality that fostered close-knit friendships. But as Linda entered middle-age, her attitude began to shift. She wanted to settle down, and she had finally found the right man.

Two years in and the relationship was solid as ever. She was a famous psychotherapist. He was an economist and triathlete. They were in love. Linda's kids had grown up and moved out. Her partner had a teenage daughter who lived with him. The plan was that once his daughter moved out, they would move in together and marry.

The day finally arrived when his daughter left for college.

A week later, Linda's partner invited her to their favorite restaurant on the coast. Linda felt giddy as she listened to the waves crashing. They ordered wine and lobster. She was starstruck all over by the handsome hunk across from her. The moment was perfect.

The waiter removed their empty dinner plates and handed them the dessert menu. Linda's partner smiled and took her hand. His grip was warm. He began to share his thoughts of their future. He was living alone for the first time in decades. He said he experienced a renewed sense of freedom. He wanted to explore this feeling of expansiveness more. Then he said he made the decision to live alone for the next few years.

Linda froze.

The agreement was that when his daughter moved out, they would move in together. Linda had invested two years of her life into this relationship waiting on that promise. Now her partner was changing the agreement. A dizzying wave of emotion passed through her. She looked at her partner, the man she was sure she would marry. He looked back at her. It suddenly felt like he was a million miles away.

What could Linda do in this situation? She could react defensively and argue. She could try to prove they were a perfect couple. She could concede and accept his terms. But Linda chose to do none of these.

Linda stared at her partner across the dinner table – her future fiancé, or so she had thought. She no longer heard the waves crashing in the background. She could no longer taste the wine. All she could think about was that he didn't want to move in together and get married. Her partner's goals were no longer in alignment with her own.

Linda paused for a long time in silence. Finally the clouds in her mind parted and she saw her way forward. She said, "You know I want to get married. Clearly you don't. Well then, I guess our relationship is over." She placed her napkin on the table, and then she stood up and walked out.

Linda's home was a couple miles away. She drove there alone.

The relationship was over. Her ex-partner made it clear he didn't have the same goals as she did. It was heartbreaking, but what could she do? Days passed, followed by sleepless nights. Linda began to refocus on her future and what she truly wanted. Then her phone rang. She picked up the receiver and said hello. A familiar husky voice responded, "Linda, will you marry me?"

Linda and her partner moved in together and went on to share many wonderful decades of marriage. Her story shows us the power of self-respect. But it touches upon something deeper – the source of that self-respect. Powerful people are self-directed. Linda had the strength to force the issue of living together by having a clear understanding of her goal. When Linda stayed true to her goal, she created the opportunity for her desired reality to exist. As Linda shared with me, it was precisely because she walked out on her partner that he was forced to consider her needs in the relationship and to confront how important the relationship was to him. The result was the life she had dreamt of.

We frequently give away our power by focusing on external achievements as a measure of our personal worth. But the more we focus externally, the more we trigger the psychology of powerlessness. Our ability to maintain boundaries and to experience fulfillment begins by anchoring in our internal goals and values. Once we are internally anchored, we communicate our power by evaluating the environment in pursuit of those goals, enhancing our power both internally and externally.

In 2011, Oprah Winfrey wrapped up her 25th and final season of *The Oprah Winfrey Show*. The show ranks as one of the 50 greatest TV shows of all time. After her final season, Oprah was interviewed on what made her show successful. She responded that when thinking about the show, she asked herself questions such as, "How do we want to see the world change? How do we want to impact the world?"[26] She focused her episodes on her answers. Oprah's perspective stands in stark contrast to the story of the failed startup Sonar at the beginning of the chapter. Whereas Sonar looked outward for guidance, especially to competition, Oprah looked inward. Oprah said she viewed competition as a motivation to focus more deeply on her own goals rather than compare herself to others.

Real success comes when you view success as arising from internal power to create external reward rather than securing external reward to create internal power. When you sacrifice your values for external gain and succeed, in the victory is still defeat. And when you sacrifice your values and fail, you're left with nothing but a wasteland on the inside and the outside. But if you maintain your inner values and fail externally, you're still left with your personal power. And like Nelson Mandela, there is every possibility you will rise again to even more extraordinary heights. Power is not about being right all the time, it's about where you put your anchor.

This brings us to the penultimate chapter to ensure your voice is heard even when others try to silence you.

The Power of Affirmation

We walk into situations that feel threatening all the time. These situations can be highly visible meetings with management, negotiations with customers, or interpersonal conflicts. It's natural to feel intimidated in these moments.

One simple way you can overcome feelings of threat is to anchor into your values. Researchers found that when negotiators tapped into their values immediately prior to a negotiation, they were more successful during the negotiation.[31]

Roughly ten minutes before you enter a high stakes situation, list out some of your most important values in life. If you have trouble coming up with a list of values, you can find a list online. I have also provided you the following list. Rank order your list from top to bottom, highest value first. Spend the next five minutes writing about why you chose your top value to be the most important value, and how that value is relevant to the situation and to your life as a whole.

The writing is the most important step. When you actively reflect on your most important value for several minutes, you anchor your mind internally. This anchor energizes your personal power. Like all exercises, this exercise only works when you do it in the moment. When you enter a different situation, repeat the process from the beginning to recondition your mind in the new moment. Here is a list of values you can use.[32]

Altruism	Harmony
Kindness	Artistry
Rationality	Influence
Search for Truth	Leadership
Resourcefulness	Holiness
Practicality	Unity

The Power of Presence and Curiosity

We may find ourselves in moments when we are harshly criticized or accused of negative behavior. The criticism could be entirely untrue, or it could be blown out of proportion. But the result damages our reputation and our relationship with others.

Obviously the first thing we should do in moments of harsh criticism or false accusation is state the truth. But after doing that, the default follow-up reaction is often to become defensive or prove our innocence. You can see how this follow-up reaction immediately backfires. Proving undermines our ability to resolve the situation because it reduces our power and thereby our ability to be heard in the situation. For example, think how being accused of theft immediately makes the accused's elaborate defense more suspicious.

One technique that is particularly useful under times of harsh criticism or false accusation is to practice presence and curiosity. Presence brings us into the moment, interrupting our unconscious reactions that lead us to become defensive. Once we are present, we can choose how to respond. A powerful response is curiosity. Curiosity puts us into learning mode where we seek information, in this case understanding the reasons for the criticism. Curiosity gives us the capability to understand the roots of the criticism and to participate in clarifying the situation.

Often in situations of heightened emotion where the criticism is false or overblown, the criticism may reflect more about the accuser than the accused. Anchored in our reality, we can be open and learn about the accuser's motivation and perspective without becoming defensive.

This learning respects the relationship and balances out the power dynamic by demonstrating our personal power.

Research suggests that when we practice presence and curiosity, we break the cycle of behavioral confirmation that sets up the accuser as evaluator and the target as guilty.[33] The next time you find yourself harshly criticized or accused of something you did not do and denial alone is insufficient to maintain trust, pause, take a breath, state your truth, and engage presence and curiosity.

You can practice presence and curiosity to interrupt the negative expectations someone projects onto you in many other situations. For example, if your manager has negative expectations of your performance, become present and curious as to what they'd like to see in your performance. In short, when you are the target of negative attention, practice PC.

8 | Speak Up

Bill and Paul are two entrepreneurs you don't know. One is balding, the other is Scottish, and between them is enough brainpower to fuel cutting-edge technology. Of the many startups they founded, "Lumin" was the most successful. At one point, Lumin boasted over 100 employees and millions of dollars in revenue. The tech company was set to compete with industry giants like Cisco. Then the founders hired the wrong CEO.

Alex was brought in to lead the company and raise money for Lumin's expansion. He was a keen salesman with a raucous laugh. Alex quickly proved his value by engaging investors and securing financial support. But for all of Alex's bluster, he was insecure. Alex wanted to be the top dog, and he viewed Bill and Paul as threats.

The reason you don't know Bill and Paul is because of how they managed Alex. The founders recognized that Alex felt threatened, so they proceeded to act intentionally non-threatening. They gave Alex every opportunity to stand center-stage. In corporate meetings, they let Alex run the show. In board meetings, the founders took a backseat and let Alex do

161

the talking. The founders hired this guy after all, they wanted him to succeed.

But Alex's insecurity ran deep. He started a smear campaign to discredit the founders. He continued to consolidate his power with the corporate board. At one point Alex attempted to cut the founders out of board meetings through a series of procedural changes. Although Bill and Paul were ultimately not barred from the board, they lost control of the company narrative. Within two years, both founders were fired. When Bill spoke to one of the board members who fired them, the board member said, "you guys were always silent in meetings, you didn't speak up much." Eventually Alex, lacking the technical expertise previously provided by founders, drove the company into the ground.

There is no world in which someone gains power without being heard. The founders of Lumin brought critically-needed value to their company. But by taking a backseat in board meetings, the founders placed their power in the hands of another and lost out.

Could they have avoided this outcome?

Be Visible

My friend Cathy works in digital marketing for a major service group. She is quiet and soft-spoken, a natural introvert. Her quietness belies her brilliance. In her first two years at the company, she increased online-driven sales revenue by several millions of dollars. But despite her success, she was shuffled under a director who pulled strings to secure the management position. Cathy's situation wasn't optimal. She had wanted the director position. The new director also didn't know the online business.

Cathy rolled with the punch. She assumed her two years at the company wasn't long enough to prove herself. She doubled down on her commitment. She taught her director about digital marketing. She continued to produce amazing results. The new director was pleased.

Cathy's next performance review came around. She was livid. Her performance was marked unexceptional, earning her only a nominal raise.

Cathy realized that every week when the director presented Cathy's data to executive leadership, the results reflected on the director. The harder Cathy worked, the more the director looked good in front of the executives. Rather than reward Cathy or share credit, the director took advantage of Cathy by keeping her down. The director even muzzled Cathy, telling her that all communication to executives had to go through the director. Like Bill and Paul, Cathy lost control of her narrative. She didn't realize this was a problem until her muted performance review. Cathy felt stuck. She either had to make her voice heard or seek out new pastures.

Cathy set up a meeting with her VP to discuss her latest data. She didn't copy the director on the invitation. The gambit worked and the two met. The VP was impressed with Cathy's results and began copying Cathy on emails. Whenever the VP emailed questions to the director and copied Cathy, Cathy responded to the VP immediately rather than wait for her director to funnel the data up.

Cathy made further effort to share data with her colleagues around the office. Public sharing ensured her knowledge remained out in the open. The director was no longer pleased, but Cathy realized the director's pleasure wasn't gaining her points in performance reviews. Because Cathy was an introvert, it was hard to put herself out there at first. She felt uncomfortable. But her actions paid off. Once Cathy's work became visible to senior management, her reputation spoke for itself. Soon Cathy was invited into executive meetings. When the director presented Cathy's data, Cathy spoke up to elaborate on various points. Cathy even left out pieces of information from her director's presentations so that Cathy's clarification was required. When Cathy spoke, she demonstrated the extent of her knowledge as well as the fact that she was the source of the data.

Within a year, Cathy was promoted to run her own team.

Research shows time and again that those with personal power speak up. Powerful people engage more in group discussions, make the opening arguments in debates, and make the first offers in negotiations.[1] Speaking up leads to outer perceptions of power.

At UC Berkeley, Cameron Anderson hosted a math competition to explore how different behaviors led to more or less power in groups.[2] Students were organized into teams of four to compete against other teams. Cameron videotaped each team as they worked together. After the competition, Cameron had students rate their teammates on math skills, social skills, and group influence.

Students who were rated highest on math and social skills by their teammates were those who spoke up most. The students who spoke up shared more information about problems and proposed more answers.* But here's the kicker – students who spoke up most weren't any better at math than their teammates. Their answers were wrong just as frequently as everyone else's. By simply volunteering more answers, students were rated higher on both math and social skills. These students also scored highest on group influence, a proxy for power.

Speaking up is the volume control to your power. The more you speak up, the more your perceived value increases. All things being equal, if you have the same ability as your peers but you volunteer more solutions to problems, you are going to be seen

---

*Speaking up was also perceived as directing the group toward a common goal. In sum, speaking up in groups was seen as the triad of creating value by addressing problems, focusing on the big picture common goal, and coordinating group activity toward that goal.

as more powerful. You turned your power volume up. This is one reason why extraverts often secure more power in groups. Being vocally outspoken is powerful.

Cameron took his research a step further. He invited research staff to watch the videos of teams working together and to rate students on their skills and influence. How did outside observers rate the students' behaviors? The staff also rated the students who spoke up most as having the most influence in the group. In other words, students who spoke up most were seen as more powerful by others both inside and outside the group.

There is a silver lining for introverts. Additional research showed that if an extravert's contribution is consistently inferior over several months' time, their status falls.[3] Speaking up cannot forever replace the need for actual quality performance. But by default, speaking up is a gateway to convey personal power.

Telling ourselves to speak up is easy, but speaking up can be hard. For example, we may worry about being wrong. But as Cameron's research showed, being right or wrong is not what makes us powerful. Our reputation isn't rooted in our accuracy, it's in our voice. Still, we may worry about being judged. So we shy away from the opportunity to speak up in the moment. We tell ourselves we'll speak up next time. But when we withhold our voice, we activate the Behavioral Inhibition System (BIS). The BIS fuels fear. When we inhibit our voice, we program the BIS to be stronger, making it less likely we will speak up the next time. We become bystanders.

Health Counselor Dr. Vassilia Binensztok gave great advice on addressing the fear of speaking up. "When you're not used to being confident, confidence feels like arrogance. When you're used to being passive, assertiveness feels like aggression. When you're not used to getting your needs met, prioritizing yourself feels selfish. Your comfort zone is not a good benchmark."[4] Discomfort is not an indicator of efficacy, it's an indicator of a shift in habit. There is no shame in feeling fear. It is reaction to fear that leads to powerlessness. A huge shift happens when we begin to see fear not as a handicap but as a doorway to expansion.

You don't need to be the loudest voice in the room nor dominate every conversation. We all know people like this – it gets annoying. But when you have something to say, say it. Stand up for your ideas. If you're not the most important person in the room, plan on being intimidated. But take your attention off your fears and focus on your goals. Anchor in your confidence knowing that you invested time and energy into your ideas and skills. You are the sponsor of your own ideas. Sometimes the difference between getting what you want and not getting what you want is simply voicing your thoughts.

After Lumin's collapse, I asked the founders what they could have done differently to protect their power around the CEO. The founders said they should have built informal relationships with the board. They could have gone to lunches or grabbed coffee with board members. These meetings would have ensured their voices were heard.

Be Authentic

It's 7pm in Austin. I'm booked in a suite in the upper floor of the Hilton downtown. It's a great pad with a couple rooms overlooking 4th Street. It's probably my third visit in as many months, and the hotel staff greet me by name. They also recognize the silver Impala that I'm driving. It was the last car on the rental lot.

SXSW starts in a couple days, it's the biggest music and media festival in the U.S. Feeling the desire to mingle with the crowd flying in for the event, I head down to the lounge on the ground floor. It's mostly empty except for a few people at the bar and a couple women in the corner. The two women are literally vibrating with giddy energy about something, so I head over and ask them what's going on. They point to the bar and tell me Robert Plant is here. Robert who. . . . The lead singer of Led Zeppelin. Wow! No wonder I couldn't get the largest suite upstairs (kidding). Suddenly I feel the giddy energy of being starstruck. It's not a deeply centering experience.

The women approach the bar and try to drag me along, but I resist. They move right up on both sides of Plant, fawning and giggling, trying to pull him into a selfie. Plant takes it totally nonchalant, apparently it goes with the business. But the guy next to him, who is easily the coolest looking dude I have ever seen, moves in. This guy is wearing five grand worth of fabric as if it's workout clothes. "Come on ladies, shows some respect," he says with a frown. And after a few more giggles, the women retreat back to where I'm standing. All the while I'm thinking to myself, Robert Plant is amazing. His voice filled my home for years, I have to say something. But at the same time, the last thing I want to do is come off as a vacuous fan.

After a few minutes, I realize that there's only one thing I really want to tell this guy. Feeling calm now, I walk over and put my hand on Robert Plant's back. He turns around, his eyebrows raised. I look him in the eye and say in full authenticity, "thank you for your music." Pause.

His face brightens and he smiles. Then he gives me a flourishing bow right there in the lounge.

Wow.

At this point, the feeling of being starstruck pummels my consciousness again, and before I lose myself and cheapen the experience, I calmly turn around and walk away.

There is a common myth that feeling powerful leads us to lose touch with ourselves. *Absolute power leads to absolute corruption*, the saying goes. But powerful people are internally driven. The more we tune into ourselves, the more personal power we experience, and vice-versa. When I tapped into my authenticity, I found myself calmly placing my hand on the back of a superstar and sharing a few honest words. Clearly my authenticity was appreciated.

Researchers at UC Berkeley were curious how authenticity influences personal power.[5,6] Through a series of surveys, they found that people who spoke up authentically felt more powerful. When we speak our minds, we strengthen our internal connection.* In addition, the researchers found that when others see us speak up authentically, they see us as more powerful. In sum, authenticity fosters personal power, and people who speak up authentically are seen as more powerful.

When an important issue comes up for discussion, share what you think. If you disagree with others, express your disagreement. Don't hide your true opinions. And don't hide who you are.

But not all self-expression is healthy, especially in the office. After clawing her way into a director position at a small media firm, Nina was finally relaxing into her job. The last year had been a challenge as she navigated divorce. While her performance in the office won accolades, her now ex-husband was hell-bent on destroying her life at home. Nina was locked in constant legal battles around child custody and asset division. It was in this firestorm that the CEO decided to pay Nina an office visit.

The CEO inquired how she was doing. He smiled as Nina shared her work updates in a very direct and methodical way. When she was done, he mentioned they needed more staff. Since the CEO knew Nina's ex-husband well, the CEO casually asked whether she'd be okay if they hired her ex-husband.

Nina did a double take. The CEO didn't wait for an answer, he smiled and walked out.

---

*Research also suggests authenticity mediates the relationship between personal power and subjective well-being. Personal power is linked to being authentic, and it is our authenticity, not our power as such, that makes us more satisfied with life.[29]

After the CEO left, Nina caught her breath. There was no way this was okay with her. She needed to find a way to convince the CEO of this. Nina spent the weekend stewing on how to deliver her message. In the end she decided full transparency was the way to go. On Monday she went to her CEO's office and shared her thoughts. Almost immediately her emotions overwhelmed her. She teared up and her voice shrilled as she described the pain her ex was causing her. Her sharing turned into a full-blown emotional meltdown.

When she walked out of his office, she knew she blew it.

The next day the CEO said she was way too emotional about this. In his mind her emotions diminished her credibility on the issue. Within the week, the CEO hired her ex. A month later, Nina requested and was granted a transfer away from headquarters to escape the situation. In my opinion, the CEO showed zero interpersonal awareness. But the point of the story is not an analysis of the CEO, it's that authenticity does not mean complete emotional transparency.

Authenticity is being true to what's relevant in the moment. Powerful people pay attention to their goals in a situation and speak up with respect to those goals. When discussing issues at work, they express their honest opinions about work. They are not focused on what's going on at home. When powerful people express their romantic feelings at home, they are not thinking about work.[7,8]

Authenticity is not expressing whatever we randomly think or feel in the moment. When we are powerless, we are easily distracted from our goals. We may be distracted by what others think of us. We may be distracted by whatever is randomly happening around us. If we were to share all these random feelings, we'd be transparent. But we would not be authentic to what's truly important for us in that moment. And where there is a lack of authenticity, there is a lack of power.

Brene Brown, one of the modern leaders in vulnerability research, cautions, "Vulnerability minus boundaries is not vulnerability. Are you sharing your emotions [and] your experiences to move [your] work, connection, or relationship forward? Or are you working your shit out with somebody? And work is not a place to do that."[9]

Nina was transparent, but sharing her personal emotions gained no traction with the CEO because it was inconsistent with the needs of business. Perhaps had she discussed how hiring her ex-husband would negatively impact team dynamics or require her to transfer (setting a boundary), the discussion would have ended differently. You choose what is relevant to your goals and values in the current environment with the current people.

One of the most common areas where we let our emotions get the better of us is anger. Anger is reactive and consuming. Anger can lead to regretful decisions. Anger can destroy relationships. But anger is associated with power under the right conditions. Researchers found that when expressing negative emotions, high-energy emotions like anger are perceived as more powerful than low-energy emotions like sadness.[10] Those who display anger over sadness convey more competence, whereas those who display sadness over anger convey more warmth. In the office, competence is key. And anger shows signs of being connected with the Behavioral Approach System, the system associated with power.[11] But anger is still a negative emotion that turns many people away. I have yet to hear a single colleague say they respected someone more because that person showed anger.*

When you feel negative emotions and anger is at the forefront, use your anger in service to a goal. Anger energizes us

---

*Anger per se is not a signal of power. For example, chronic anger is associated with low status.[30] And we are all familiar with feeling simultaneously angry and helpless.

to overcome challenges and resistance. In negotiation, anger directed at another person can result in worse outcomes. But anger directed at unfair offers can result in greater negotiation outcomes.[12] Don't make anger personal, make it about your goals and boundaries. High-power individuals use their emotions to achieve goals, whereas low-power individuals are used by their emotions. Recognize that when negative emotions arise, it's always important to stay focused on the goal.

It was a late summer afternoon, and Mitch was roasting in the meeting room. The sun blazed through the windows as the discussion dragged on. Mitch's only thought was to get out of that room and head down to the local pub. But this was an important software meeting. People from sales, marketing, service, and development were sitting at the table. There were around 10 people in total, all mid-level and senior management. Mitch was the head of product marketing. He wasn't the most important person in the room, that was probably the VP of Sales.

Leading the discussion was Dr. Paul from development. Paul was a bit of an intellectual elitist and passive-aggressive in his comments. Whenever someone shared an idea Paul didn't like, Paul spent a few minutes criticizing the idea. These criticisms kept the meeting dragging. After a sales director finished sharing some new thoughts, Paul launched into another two-minute diatribe against what had been said.

For Mitch, sitting there dripping sweat, this was too much. Mitch interrupted, "Paul, we're all trying to get things done and do our best. Your behavior is critical and irritating and not conducive to an easy outcome. Will you please be more cooperative and try to give more positive comments?" Mitch wasn't Paul's superior, they weren't even in the same division. It didn't matter. After Mitch spoke, Paul became a lamb. The meeting moved smoothly for another 30 minutes before they adjourned to the local pub.

Mitch's words weren't a personal attack on Paul, Mitch was merely voicing what he felt and what he believed others were feeling too. And Paul didn't take it personally. Mitch's comments focused on the behavior, not the person.

Be Certain and Decisive

The halogen lights glared off the white bedsheets as the orthopedic physician stepped into my room. His assistant trailed behind and positioned herself in the corner with a clipboard. A day at the gym the month prior had given me an aching shoulder injury that refused to heal. I had no idea what was wrong, but the injury burned deep beneath the surface. The physician walked over to where I sat, his white hair glinting in the light. Clearly he'd been at this job a long time.

I quickly summarized my pain. He nodded, then signaled me to raise my arm. Pain? No. He took my arm and maneuvered it through a few other movements. Pain? No. Pain? Yes! I winced, feeling electricity shoot down my arm. He nodded and mumbled some lingo to his assistant that sounded like subscapularis and pectoralis minor. Then he prodded his fingers into my shoulder. Ouch! I heard more jargon to the assistant. He looked at me, "it's a muscle injury where the shoulder attaches to the chest. We need to determine if you tore it or not. We'll schedule an MRI and have you come back to discuss next steps." I asked a few questions, then the appointment was over. The whole ordeal took no more than 10 minutes. Normally when doctors swoop in and out quickly, I feel like I'm on the conveyor belt of institutionalized medicine. But not this time.

The physician didn't spend time joking or chatting, he simply did a few tests and spoke directly to my issue. When I asked questions, he listened and gave direct answers. Once he made a clear diagnosis of the problem, he made a decisive recommendation. I left feeling completely satisfied because this physician knew exactly what I was feeling and exactly what he was doing to solve my problem. The doctor was powerful.

One hallmark of powerful communication is certainty. A group of researchers led out of UNC found that courtroom witnesses were seen as more powerful and more credible when speaking without the use of hedge words or hesitation.[13] Most of us use hedge words all the time to convey uncertainty in our thoughts. We say words like, "I think" or "I believe" or "kind of." But my doctor didn't say, "I think maybe this is a muscle injury," which sounds uncertain and weak, my doctor stated his conclusion as a fact. Because those who feel powerful trust their thinking, they are more likely to state their thoughts as facts without hedging.

Another way we convey uncertainty is through embolalia, or filler words. Saying words like "umm," "uh," and "so" conveys hesitation. This is why when you hear someone say, "So, umm I think maybe it's a uh muscle injury and you should umm, get it checked out, don't you think?" The natural response is, no thank you!

Certainty goes hand-in-hand with decisiveness, and decisiveness is power. Ana Guinote conducted a study in England where students were made to feel either powerful or powerless. Ana then asked students how long they would need to shop for a car or decide where to travel next summer.[14] She discovered that students who felt powerful needed significantly less time to come to a decision than their powerless peers. The powerless were less decisive and procrastinated before taking action. Once my doctor made his diagnosis, he immediately scheduled the next step to get an MRI. His focus on next steps gave me confidence that I was on the path to healing. Powerful people are quicker to commit to action.

Be Firm and Direct

Martha Jeong reached out to people on Craigslist to see who
would give her the best discount on a used iPhone. Definitely my
type of person. I enjoy negotiating the purchase of retail goods.
It's a great opportunity to test different persuasion methods. For
example, sometimes I highlight similarities between the seller and
me. Sometimes I point out flaws in the product. I practice these
techniques a couple times each month. But Martha put my efforts
to shame. She and her colleagues at Harvard reached out to over
700 sellers to identify the best way to score a good deal.[15]

Martha sent messages to sellers that were either warm and
friendly or firm and direct. For example,

> Warm: *Hello! I liked your listing . . . Would you be willing to accept
> 80% of the listed price?*
> Firm: *I saw your post about the phone . . . I'm willing to pay 80% of
> the listed price.*

This experiment was one of several that Martha conducted
to explore how warm communication differs from firm communication in negotiation. Martha had already asked a group of
random people whether the warm or firm messages would be
more effective before reaching out to iPhone sellers. Everyone
agreed that warm messages would work better.

But they were all wrong.

Sellers consistently gave steeper discounts to firm messages.
This was true regardless of whether the item being purchased was
an iPhone or a glass bowl. Firm messages were seen as stronger.

Many times we lean into warm language to make others feel
better about the transaction. We want to be friendly. However,
sellers in Martha's experiment did not report more enjoyment
dealing with warm people. Warmth was irrelevant to sellers. And
we're not talking about the opinion of one or two people. We're
talking about hundreds of people.

Sometimes we lean into warm language out of politeness. Politeness ensures that social interactions flow smoothly. Politeness can also signal that we respect the position of the other person. But being chronically polite without signaling power conveys that others have power over us.[16] Being firm is not being rude. Think about firmness as, "to the point." Powerful people's first priority is not to be liked, it's to achieve a goal.

You may be a person who deeply values people. I do. What makes you a good person in many situations is upholding your value of people, not the warmth of your speech. We don't find comfort at work in the warmth of each other's words, we find comfort in achieving a shared purpose. When you are firm and direct with your values, you promote your values.

Don't be artificially warm, be true to yourself. Warmth is unrelated to power. With that in mind, let's turn to a topic long overdue for discussion.

Dominance

Bill Gates launched the Microsoft empire in 1975. A little over a decade later he became the youngest billionaire in the world. Today we associate Bill with philanthropy through the Gates Foundation, but his corporate heyday showed him to be a dominator. At Microsoft, he habitually used profanity and cursed his employees' work.[17] When Bill read specs for new products, he asked increasingly difficult questions until the development teams no longer had answers. Then he would berate the team for their lack of preparation.[18] But society doesn't regard Bill Gates as ruthless. If anything, many see him as an icon. There is very little negative stigma associated with Bill's leadership style, which is strange because we frequently condemn dominance.

Dominance is the act of disempowering others. It is the flip side of power. Take everything you learned in this book, turn it around, and use it as a weapon to diminish the power of others. That's dominance. Examples of dominance include devaluing the contributions of others, using your agenda to silence others, and steamrolling over others' boundaries. At a more fundamental level, dominance instills fear in others, and fear is the hallmark of the low-power mindset.[19] Fear disconnects people from their internal anchors so they become reactive to (ratify) the dominator. In this way, the dominator gains power not necessarily by standing taller than everyone, but by cutting others down so others stand lower.*

Researchers on the East Coast sought to understand how most people view dominance at work.[20] The researchers invited participants to read a scenario in which two colleagues vied for status over one-another. When one colleague tried to dominate the other, participants saw the behavior as self-serving. The participants recommended the dominator be punished. Nobody likes dominance. Researchers took the experiment a step further and had the person being dominated lash back with their own dominant behavior. In other words, when one colleague tried to dominate the other, the other colleague defended themselves by acting counter-dominant. When participants read about the counter-dominator, they also recommended the counter-dominator be punished. When someone acts dominant, regardless of whether they initiate or react with it, they are viewed negatively.

Then the researchers did something unique. They altered the scenario so that one colleague tried to dominate the other not to enhance their own personal status, but to better serve the group's goals. Would this change how their dominant behaviors were viewed?

When participants read about dominators acting in service to the group, they recommended the dominator be *rewarded*.

Why do we respect some dominators and disrespect others? Why do we respect Bill Gates but view Harvey Weinstein as anathema? In simplest terms, dominance is a self-assertive act that can be used to serve the group.

---

*Many behaviors linked to exclusion, including microaggressions and status conflicts, are acts of dominance.[31]

Those with a strong sense of personal power, the same people who take responsibility and act courageously, may naturally convey dominance at times.[21] Great leaders use dominance to focus the group, to push others to do their best, and to silence time-wasters. Coming from the big picture, a leader understands when to use dominance as a means to achieving a goal.

Engineers working for Bill Gates said that although the experience was challenging, the opportunity to push their limits and create great products was worth it.[22] Bill Gates remains an icon of leadership precisely because he led Microsoft to achieve great things on a monumental scale. Many of Bill's fellow dominators like Steve Jobs and Andy Grove remain icons because they too used dominance to produce results that served everyone, including the very people they dominated.

Dominance is also a way to maintain the status quo. Hierarchies operate effectively because of structure, and desire for structure is innate in human psychology. Once groups settle into hierarchies, combative behavior between members drops significantly. In other words, groups work together more effectively when there is order.[23] The military is a prime example of the necessity of a chain of command to avoid chaos. In the military, insubordination is punished harshly because it undermines the group. What this means professionally is that it's never okay to dominate one's superiors. Avoid putting them into the position where they have to prove themselves to you or where they fear you. It is the role and responsibility of superiors to protect against threats to the structure. Not to mention that nobody likes being dominated, and those with formal power will feel compelled to retaliate against threats to their authority.

While dominance has a positive side, research on dominance suggests that dominant behavior in service to the group is still not valued as much as conveying positive personal power.[24] Increasing your own power in service to the group is more valued than diminishing the power of others in service to the group. Years later after retiring from Microsoft, Bill Gates confided that pushing too hard too often was counterproductive.[25] Bill said he pushed hard because he felt there was never a moment to waste. Under the pressure of an impending deadline, dominance can be an efficient tool to motivate groups quickly. Dominance keeps people in line and gets things done. But people don't function well under the constant stress of feeling that there's not enough time. Stress causes burnout. Bill reflected that long term capability was more important than chronic short-term output.

Where dominance goes truly wrong is when it's used to serve the dominator's ego. Dominators may act dominant to secure power for the sake of power or simply to harm others. No one values this behavior. When a leader maintains their status through dominance without providing value to the group, the fear they create must be continually reinforced.[26] Without the fear, there is nothing to keep others in line. Thus, dominance only works to the degree others participate in being dominated. The power derived from egocentric dominance doesn't rest with the self, it rests outside the self. Such behavior is not only deeply loathed, it is unsustainable. If we dominate others in order to win approval or combat feelings of insecurity, we're not only going to alienate those around us, we're going to alienate ourselves. When we react to our insecurity by acting dominant, we diminish our feelings of personal power on the inside, spiraling us into feeling even less power. There is a reason personal power is not correlated with exploitation and entitlement.[27] Self-serving dominance is often dressed-up low-power behavior.[28]

That is why, throughout this book, you have learned ways to reinforce your own power in the face of dominance. Nowhere is it more important to protect your power than when facing those who seek to disempower you. When someone tries to dominate you, first and foremost do not react. You do not need to take their aggression as a threat. Stay anchored internally in your goals, not in their external opinions. When you stay anchored internally, you are able to maintain your boundaries and your perspective. Your boundaries reflect your self-respect. And when you don't react, you don't ratify their behavior. By maintaining your power in the face of dominating threats, regardless of whether you "win" the situation, you gain immense respect from both the dominator and those watching.

Don't Wait to be Seen

No one is paying attention to me! my friend lamented about her work. She believed her Master's degree was insufficient for gaining attention and recognition in the corporate world. She asked me if she should go back to school and get a PhD. This is a common question I hear from people who feel stuck. I told her that getting a degree to win more attention seemed like an expensive way to prove herself. She was waiting to be heard, waiting to be recognized. People who wait often end up waiting more until they lose patience and move on. These people will change jobs or get an advanced degree. But after entering the workforce in a new company or a new team, they quickly end up waiting again. The issue is not about earning a better degree or waiting for someone to see us.

We often hear stories of individuals going off alone and having their *aha!* moment. Great leaders and messiahs who went up a hill and had their brilliant insight. Moses, Jesus, Mohammad, the Buddha, Nelson Mandela, Gandhi, MLK, and on and on. But it wasn't their moment on the hill that made them great. Their greatness arose after they came down the hill and engaged others.

Our voice is our ultimate power. To be seen, we need to speak up. Speaking up is the gateway that allows us to show up. There can be no self-expression without expressing ourselves. In a world where everything feels superficial, authenticity is your secret sauce. Authenticity arises from being tapped into your thoughts and values. And when powerful people speak, they speak directly to the issue at hand. Their words are direct and decisive. To be powerful, honor your voice.

The Power of Group Affirmation

We are not always the ingroup. Oprah said that she'd frequently be the only Black woman sitting in a room full of White men. In these situations, Oprah reminded herself that she was not alone in that room, that she stood with the thousands of women who came before her and forged the path to her seat.[32]

Research suggests group affirmation can buffer our self-esteem against discrimination and similar threats to our identity. When you are the minority or you feel unaccepted because of some trait related to your identity, you can tap into the power of the group that stands with you.

A few minutes before you enter a potentially difficult situation, follow the instructions below to strengthen your inner connection. These instructions are taken straight from the research:

> "Think about a group of people with whom you feel very close and share common goals. Please write down the first group of this kind that comes to mind." Examples might be a club you belong to, a group of friends, or a spiritual community. After you choose a group, "read through a list of 12 values [below] and [select] the 3 values most important to that group." Next, "write a minimum of three paragraphs describing the group, the group's three important values (providing concrete examples of how the group has demonstrated the values . . .), and why belonging to the group was important to [you]."[33]

Do not wait for the world to change and make you feel comfortable. You are the person who will change the world by tapping into your personal power.[34]

Here is the list of values to choose from:

Artistic skills/aesthetic appreciation	Honesty/open communication
Sense of humor	Physical fitness/health
Loyalty/commitment	Sharing/giving
Music ability/appreciation	Spirituality/faith
Political activism	Volunteerism
Spontaneity/living life in the moment	Support/encouragement

9 | Epilogue

"They're after me. Help me or I'll kill you!" The hulking 6-foot man stood in the doorway to the classroom. He was shirtless with a crazed look in his eyes. His words echoed into the ears of twelve preschool children and one very young teacher named Mandy.

Mandy received an invitation to substitute teach at the Montessori school that morning. She is a gentle woman with a radiant smile. She is also my mother. Mandy previously owned the preschool, but she sold the school to be a stay-at-home parent. Who could blame her for wanting to be with her little angels? The new school owner invited Mandy to substitute when teaching staff was short. Mandy hadn't taught for about six months, but she was happy to head in that day. The morning and lunch went along without incident.

After lunch, Mandy got the twelve children in her classroom bedded down on their mats for a nap. She was sitting between two children rubbing their backs when she heard a scream. The front door slammed. Then another scream and another slam. She sat puzzled and waiting. Later she learned that two other teachers were approached in their classrooms and threatened, and they escaped the building.

The man who threatened the teachers now entered Mandy's room. He weighed 275 lbs to her 110 lbs. Physically there was no contest. He saw her on the floor and started toward her. She sat staring as he approached, and she felt the air get very warm. He stopped about five feet away. She was alone now in the school with a total of 42 children across three classrooms and a giant standing before her.

She spoke calmly, "What can I do for you?"

"They're after me. Help me or I'll kill you!" he screamed.

"Who is after you?" she asked.

"The police!"

At that moment, Mandy registered the blare of sirens. Glancing out of the window, she saw six police cars. The school was surrounded. The man eyed the back door and started toward it, nearly stepping on a child.

Mandy got up and took his hand. "Wait, I'll help you," she said. She could feel him calm down. A moment later, two policemen burst through the back door. The man became more agitated, glancing at the police and then the children.

Mandy turned to the officers and spoke, "Officers, you won't hurt him, will you?"

"No," they responded.

Still holding the giant man's hand, she walked him over to the officers. The man followed along docilely. The police took the man's arms and escorted him out of the school.

The other two teachers and the director returned to the school. They were hysterical. The director had been the first to leave when she was accosted in the front office. She had run down the street in search of a policeman. Finding one had not been difficult in downtown.

When an officer came back to finish his report, Mandy learned that the man had escaped from the mental health care unit of a nearby detention facility. The officer suggested that the director talk to her teachers as they should not have run out of the school, leaving "the little teacher all alone with 42 children." That said, Mandy didn't feel so little at the time.

Mandy's situation represents the very worst we might encounter in a day's work. Stories of school massacres are a terrible legacy of America today. Having a woman like Mandy protect our children is exactly what we need in society. Most of us would call Mandy's actions courageous, but Mandy wouldn't use that word to describe what she herself felt.

When Mandy faced the man, she knew she was responsible for the children in the school. Although the other teachers panicked under threat, Mandy instinctively dropped deep into herself. Her feelings arose to meet the necessity of the moment. She focused on protecting the children while extending a level of support to the man.

The psychology of personal power is rooted in a feeling of control, an internal orientation, and a focus on action. This first triad is the foundation for courage. When we tap into these roots of power, we naturally radiate an aura that others respond to. The man who broke into the school found himself face-to-face not with a woman half his size, but with another human rooted in her power. He was unconsciously influenced to respond to that power.

Our social power is rooted in serving others. Those who secure senior positions in hierarchies are those who provide the most value to the group. The group is merely a collection of individuals. When you serve the individuals in the group, they hold you in esteem. Power is not power over others. Power is not a goal. Power is a consequence of providing value. Of service. Mandy reached out to the aggressor in service. Service was how a woman physically half the size of a man wielding brute force was able to direct the man's behavior.

Mandy also responded to the big picture of the situation. At the concrete level, she faced off against a clear physical threat. But at the abstract level, she was the protector of the school's children. Getting to the heart of the matter wasn't about zooming in on the threat, it was about focusing on her role in the wider situation. Her perspective informed her behavior.

Finally, when the police arrived, Mandy took control of the interaction between the police and the man. She briefly controlled the agenda. Managing the situation allowed her to hand the man over to police care without incident. Serving others, seeing the big picture, and managing the situation make up the second triad of personal power focused on delivering value.

At each step in this story, Mandy radiated power.

Power Today

Everybody is born with the same capability for personal power. Like physical health and self-esteem, power is fundamental to the human experience. And power is linked to feeling happier and optimistic. You do not need to wait for someone or something outside you to help you access your power. You can claim that power residing within yourself right now. And you can use your power to help others find theirs.

In modern society, disempowerment is a reality for many individuals through absolutely no fault of their own. Research from MIT suggests that people raised in lower social economic status have chronically lower activation of the Behavioral Approach System, the brain circuits of personal power.[1] And many of the actions associated with exclusion are acts of disempowerment.[2]

If we cannot perceive our own power, we cannot conceive of our opportunity and responsibility to use it. Each of us is afforded a certain level of power that is factually available to us in society. For example, almost all adult citizens in the United States have the right to vote.[3] And yet, those who feel disempowered are less likely to believe their vote counts, and thus are less motivated to go out and actually vote. Many individuals who commit acts of emotional violence are those who do not perceive the power they hold. Consider the example of abusive parents who, feeling powerless, scathingly criticize their children. Because these parents believe their words are powerless, they cannot conceive nor take responsibility for the very real consequences those words have on their children.

When you stand in your power, you become an asset to those around you. This is how humans are built – the more empowered the individual, the more empowered the team becomes, and vice-versa. While much of today's education focuses on how to create organizational change to empower teams, you as the individual are the biggest change-maker.

When you stoke your personal power, you are like a wooden log blazing with inner fire. Every log, every person, has the capacity to burn bright. As others lean in and feel your heat, they too find their flames more quickly. Thus a single empowered individual becomes the spark that lights up a team, and sometimes lights up a nation. In this way, your expression of personal power creates a cascade of positive influence that benefits society.

Ultimately all outside change starts within you. Personal power is your feeling about your own capability to create impact. Power is a state of being. Power starts as an experience on the inside, not a situation on the outside. High-power people are goal-focused, low-power people are focused on what others think of them. If you are more focused on what others think of you rather than what you believe internally, you are looking the wrong way. The good news is that the first step back to your power begins with a mere shift in attention. And one way to shift attention is to practice the third triad of power.

Asserting Ourselves

The third and final triad of power is self-assertion. This triad requires that we practice self-respect by upholding our boundaries, we practice self-direction in what we think and value, and we practice self-expression in what we say. Said another way, self-assertion means we have clarity of our present experience, inner convictions, principles, and beliefs; and we feel capable of expressing them. Let's conclude with a simple story that displays these qualities at home around the people we love.

Nathan arrived in his hometown during the German winter. Snow covered the ground, making a stark contrast to the California climate he left days before. Years had passed since his last family reunion. He stepped indoors, hung his scarf, and joined his siblings at the stout wooden dinner table. Around the table sat Nathan's three older brothers, two sisters, and a smattering of spouses. Chief among the group and dominating the conversation was Nathan's eldest brother Peter. Peter was a doctor by day and a professed narcissist by night. He was already deep into his wine by the time Nathan arrived.

After Nathan sat down, the conversation turned toward their elder sister Rose. Rose was the patron saint of the family. She regularly volunteered as a social worker to support people going through terrible situations. What made Rose so saintly was the open-hearted way she showed kindness through her words and actions. As she shared her recent social work, she began to cite Jesus' Sermon on the Mount, "Blessed are the poor in spirit, for theirs is the kingdom of heaven."[4]

It was in the middle of this sharing Peter retorted that Rose didn't serve the poor, she served the stupid. He implied that Rose was also stupid for working with them.

We are, most of us, intimately familiar with family reunions. In spite of our normal adult behavior, we fall quickly into old family roles around the dinner table. We react the same way to each other as we did in the past, caught in a powerless self-fulfilling prophecy. Nathan was the youngest of the group, and although he was an extravert, childhood conditioning had taught him to stay silent around his siblings. As a result, Nathan tolerated decades of listening to Peter berate his sisters.

But this day something inside Nathan compelled him to speak up. He turned to Peter and said, "this is mean to anybody, but how can you be so mean to your sister? You don't even understand that blessing."

And then a funny thing happened. The energy around the table shifted.

Peter immediately quieted down. He stopped dominating the conversation. The rest of the family began to share their recent lives without the constant barrage of criticism. And that evening became a much more idyllic, if unique, family gathering.

Years later, everyone in the family still remembers that evening Nathan spoke up. Although Peter's normal personality didn't improve, the dynamic between Peter and Nathan shifted. Nathan stepped out of the younger brother role and spoke up authentically. This wasn't a case of Nathan being aggressive and chaffing at the existing family dynamic, which would have been a reaction. This was a man who spoke up for his values. Authenticity seeks no approval.

The Power of Your Own Practice

Throughout this book were formal exercises based on research to help you access your personal power. But there are many practices that only you know work for you.

I find the simplest activities plug me back into myself – a walk outdoors, the smell of the evening air, listening to uplifting music. My most powerful practice is Vipassana meditation. Vipassana teaches how to tune into one's senses and feel everything arising in the body without reacting to it. I can think of no single practice that has had a more positive impact on my life than Vipassana.

Pay attention to what plugs you into you. Maybe it's sports or reading. Maybe it's breath exercises or chanting. Many powerful practices put us into our bodies, facilitating inner connection. Everyone has their own practices. But their practices are not yours. Choose what works for you and stick with what works. You will feel when it's right.

Best wishes.

Acknowledgments

My interest in personal power began with my close friend, Atashi Basu. During our late night dinners alongside another close friend, Emmanuel Mayssat, we waxed about how to convey power in the office in order to succeed. I continued these discussions with my close friends Antoine de Morree and Nik Jewell, both of whom share a similar interest and provided a huge dose of motivation for me to look deeper into the field.

I was lucky in three regards when I began. First, almost all books on power dismissed speech, and those that covered speaking with power did so very generically. As a lifelong student of persuasion, I found this untenable. Second, power for the sake of power is so empty a feeling that it did not resonate with my personal growth practice. That's no surprise given that desiring power for the sake of power is an indicator of low personal power. So I wanted to understand how to feel great on the inside and succeed on the outside simultaneously. And third, I was turned onto the work of Dacher Keltner at UC Berkeley. After listening to Dacher speak and subsequently interviewing him, I had my introduction into the field of personal power.

My deep-hearted appreciation goes out to my early readers, including Bob Lipp (Dad), Merve Aker, Andreas Sundquist,

Antoine de Morree, Bill Pierce, and Loretta Sparks. Alongside these readers are all the people who supported me in writing this book, including Angie Ni, Catherine Pierson, Elizabeth Triplett, Mandy Barber (Mom), Sehin Belew, Ashley Nelson, Nick Thomas, Emmie Thomas, Matt Abrahams, and Indigo Wong.

Some of the best stories and advice came from the people I interviewed. These include Dacher Keltner, Tracy Colwell, Reggie DesRoches, Bill Colton, Jim Hennessy, and Maggie Neale. I am equally grateful to all the people I didn't name who shared their stories with me. Your show of personal power is now an inspiration to me and to others. This demonstrates how a single act of personal power spreads to empower us all.

Special thanks to the amazing researchers whose shoulders this book stands on. While there are many, I'd like to extend thanks to Cameron Anderson, Ana Guinote, Deborah Gruenfeld, Leigh Tost, Adam Galinsky, Joe Magee, Pamela Smith, Derek Rucker, Larissa Tiedens, Pablo Briñol, Corinne Bendersky, Gerben Van Kleef, David Dubois, Vanessa Patrick, David Owens, Jeannie Kahwajy, Joris Lammers, Jeffrey Pfeffer, John Copeland, and at least two dozen others I did not mention. The pioneers of the field.

I am exceptionally grateful to the staff at Wiley. Thank you Jeanenne Ray for taking the leap to support personal power. Thank you Casper Barbour and Michelle Hacker for your excellent support. I am grateful for my editors David Schweidel, Kim Wimpsett, and Martin Tribe. And thank you to those who supported the book along the way to becoming published, including Reina Hallab, Bradley Warshaw, and Ashley Mansour.

To my teachers who are no longer here, including Nathaniel Branden and S.N. Goenka. The life lessons they taught are integrated into the fabric of my motivation, and no doubt contributed to this creation. And to those who are still here, including Anand Mehrotra.

Finally, my thanks to JD Schramm, to whom this book is dedicated. JD is singularly responsible for opening the doors that led me into my current career. He was the first to see that a young engineering/psychology graduate years ago could coach others on public speaking. He introduced me to many teachers and taught me lessons that are now so internally integrated that I see those teachings as my own. He's also a great friend with superb values, and a model for what it means to live a fulfilling life.

Notes

Chapter 1

1. Pat Gelsinger, *The Juggling Act: Bringing Balance to Your Faith, Family, and Work* (David C. Cook, 2008).
2. "Andrew Grove," Wikipedia, January 26, 2024, https://en.wikipedia.org/wiki/Andrew_Grove. Accessed 14 March 2024.
3. Kevin and Jackie Freiberg, "20 Reasons Why Herb Kelleher Was One of the Most Beloved Leaders of Our Time," *Forbes*, January 4, 2019, https://www.forbes.com/sites/kevinandjackiefreiberg/2019/01/04/20-reasons-why-herb-kelleher-was-one-of-the-most-beloved-leaders-of-our-time/. Accessed 14 March 2024.
4. Matt Blitz - TodayIFoundOut.com, "How an Arm Wrestle Resolved a Major Airline Dispute," *Gizmodo*, February 21, 2014, https://gizmodo.com/how-an-arm-wrestle-resolved-a-major-airline-dispute-1527658365. Accessed 14 March 2024.
5. Cameron Anderson et al., "Who Attains Social Status? Effects of Personality and Physical Attractiveness in Social Groups," *Journal of Personality and Social Psychology* 81, no. 1 (July 2001): 116–132.

6. Oliver P. John and Sanjay Srivastava, "The Big Five Trait Taxonomy: History, Measurement, and Theoretical Perspectives," in *Handbook of Personality: Theory and Research,* eds. Oliver P. John and Richard W. Robins (New York: Guilford Press, 1999), 2nd ed., p121.

7. Jessa Pangilinan, "27 Famous Introverts Who Had Amazing Success in Life," *Happier Human,* January 24, 2023, https://www.happierhuman.com/famous-introverts. Accessed 14 March 2024.

8. Dacher Keltner, Deborah H. Gruenfeld, and Cameron Anderson, "Power, Approach, and Inhibition," *Psychological Review* 110, no. 2 (April 2003): 265–284.

9. Cameron Anderson, Oliver P. John, and Dacher Keltner, "The Personal Sense of Power," *Journal of Personality* 80, no. 2 (February 2012): 313–344.

10. Joris Lammers et al., "Power Gets the Job: Priming Power Improves Interview Outcomes," *Journal of Experimental Social Psychology* 49, no. 4 (July 2013): 776–779.

11. Adam D. Galinsky, Derek D. Rucker, and Joe C. Magee, "Power: Past Findings, Present Considerations, and Future Directions," in *APA Handbook of Personality and Social Psychology, Vol. 3. Interpersonal Relations,* eds. Mario Mikulincer and Phillip R. Shaver (Washington, DC: American Psychological Association, 2015), p421–460.

12. Dacher Keltner, Deborah H. Gruenfeld, and Cameron Anderson, "Power, Approach, and Inhibition," *Psychological Review* 110, no. 2 (April 2003): 265–284.

13. Derek D. Rucker and Adam D. Galinsky, "Conspicuous Consumption versus Utilitarian Ideals: How Different Levels of Power Shape Consumer Behavior," *Journal of Experimental Social Psychology* 45, no. 3 (May 2009): 549–555.

14. Aaron De Smet et al., "Some Employees Are Destroying Value. Others Are Building It. Do You Know the Difference?," *McKinsey Quarterly,* September 11, 2023,

https://www.mckinsey.com/capabilities/people-and-organizational-performance/our-insights/some-employees-are-destroying-value-others-are-building-it-do-you-know-the-difference.

Additional Reading

Scott A. Reid and Sik Hung Ng, "Language, Power, and Intergroup Relations," *Journal of Social Issues* 55, no. 1 (January 1999): 119–139.

Paul Julian Smith and Wilhelm Hofmann, "Power in Everyday Life," *Proceedings of the National Academy of Sciences of the United States of America* 113, no. 36 (August 2016): 10043–10048.

Chapter 2

1. Robert Iger, *The Ride of a Lifetime: Lessons Learned from 15 Years as CEO of the Walt Disney Company* (Random House, 2019).

2. "George Washington and the Cherry Tree (U.S. National Park Service)," n.d., https://www.nps.gov/articles/george-washington-and-the-cherry-tree.htm. Accessed 14 March 2024.

3. Fiona Lee and Larissa Z. Tiedens, "Who's Being Served? 'Self-Serving' Attributions in Social Hierarchies," *Organizational Behavior and Human Decision Processes* 84, no. 2 (March 2001): 254–287.

4. Nathanael J. Fast et al., "Illusory Control," *Psychological Science* 20, no. 4 (April, 2009): 502–508.

5. Jen Wieczner, "Elon Musk Admits Mistakes Were Made on the Road to Tesla's Model 3," *Fortune*, June 8, 2017, https://fortune.com/2017/06/07/tesla-model-3-elon-musk-2.

6. Cameron Anderson, Oliver P. John, and Dacher Keltner, "The Personal Sense of Power," *Journal of Personality* 80, no. 2 (February 2012): 313–344.

7. Peter Belmi and Jeffrey Pfeffer, "Power and Death: Mortality Salience Increases Power Seeking While Feeling Powerful Reduces Death Anxiety," *Journal of Applied Psychology* 101, no. 5 (January 2016): 702–720.

8. Robert Iger, *The Ride of a Lifetime: Lessons Learned from 15 Years as CEO of the Walt Disney Company* (Random House, 2019). p21.

9. Gerben A. Van Kleef et al., "Power and Emotion in Negotiation: Power Moderates the Interpersonal Effects of Anger and Happiness on Concession Making," *European Journal of Social Psychology* 36, no. 4 (July 2006): 557–581.

10. Ibid., 36

11. Adam D. Galinsky et al., "Power Reduces the Press of the Situation: Implications for Creativity, Conformity, and Dissonance," *Journal of Personality and Social Psychology* 95, no. 6 (January 2008): 1450–1466.

12. Leigh Plunkett Tost, "When, Why, and How Do Powerholders 'Feel the Power'? Examining the Links between Structural and Psychological Power and Reviving the Connection between Power and Responsibility," *Research in Organizational Behavior* 35 (January 2015): 29–56.

13. Oscar Raymundo, "What Joanna Hoffman Told Kate Winslet While Shooting the 'Steve Jobs' Movie," *Macworld*, January 9, 2023, https://www.macworld.com/article/226727/what-joanna-hoffman-told-kate-winslet-while-shooting-the-steve-jobs-movie.html.

14. Laura Dang, "Meet the Woman Who Won Awards for Standing up to Steve Jobs," *NextShark*, December 19, 2021, https://nextshark.com/joanna-hoffman-steve-jobs-apple. Accessed 14 March 2024.

15. Adam D. Galinsky, Deborah H. Gruenfeld, and Joe C. Magee, "From Power to Action," *Journal of Personality and Social Psychology* 85, no. 3 (January 2003): 453–466.

16. Joe C. Magee, "From action to power: the use of action-orientation in inferences of power," (PhD diss., Stanford University, 2004).

17. Dacher Keltner, Deborah H. Gruenfeld, and Cameron Anderson, "Power, Approach, and Inhibition," *Psychological Review* 110, no. 2 (April 2003): 265–284.

18. Brett and Kate McKay, "General Patton's Strategy for Winning in War and Life: Keep Punching," *The Art of Manliness*, September 25, 2021, https://www.artofmanliness.com/character/manly-lessons/general-pattons-strategy-for-winning-in-war-and-life-keep-punching. Accessed 14 March 2024.

19. Eduardo Medina, "As a Woman Was Raped, Train Riders Failed to Intervene, Police Say," *The New York Times*, October 22, 2021, https://www.nytimes.com/2021/10/17/us/riders-watched-woman-raped-septa.html.

20. "Bystander Effect," *Wikipedia*, January 18, 2024, https://en.wikipedia.org/wiki/Bystander_effect. Accessed 14 March 2024.

21. Pauline Schilpzand, David R. Hekman, and Terence R. Mitchell, "An Inductively Generated Typology and Process Model of Workplace Courage," *Organization Science* 26, no. 1 (February 2015): 52–77.

22. Cameron Anderson, Oliver P. John, and Dacher Keltner, "The Personal Sense of Power," *Journal of Personality* 80, no. 2 (February 2012): 334.

23. "Reinforcement Sensitivity Theory," *Wikipedia*, February 19, 2024, https://en.wikipedia.org/wiki/Reinforcement_sensitivity_theory. Accessed 14 March 2024.

24. Roy F. Baumeister et al., "Who's in Charge Here?," *Personality and Social Psychology Bulletin* 14, no. 1 (March 1988): 17–22.

25. "Milgram Experiment," *Wikipedia*, February 21, 2024, https://en.wikipedia.org/wiki/Milgram_experiment. Accessed 14 March 2024.

26. Khristopher J. Brooks, "Discrimination, Race, Law, Employment Discrimination, Racism, Workplace, Ageism, Gender, Sexism," *CBS News*, October 23, 2019, https://www.cbsnews.com/news/nearly-60-of-us-workers-say-they-seen-or-experienced-discrimination-at-their-job.

Additional Reading

Stéphane Côté et al., "Social Power Facilitates the Effect of Prosocial Orientation on Empathic Accuracy," *Journal of Personality and Social Psychology* 101, no. 2 (January 2011): 217–232.

Judith A. Hall et al., "Attributing the Sources of Accuracy in Unequal-Power Dyadic Communication: Who Is Better and Why?," *Journal of Experimental Social Psychology* 42, no. 1 (January 2006): 18–27.

Yuwei Jiang, Lingjing Zhan, and Derek D. Rucker, "Power and Action Orientation: Power as a Catalyst for Consumer Switching Behavior," *Journal of Consumer Research* 41, no. 1 (June 2014): 183–96.

Chapter 3

1. "History of Italian Americans in Boston," *Wikipedia*, January 14, 2024, https://en.wikipedia.org/wiki/History_of_Italian_Americans_in_Boston. Accessed 14 March 2024.

2. William Foote Whyte, *Street Corner Society: The Social Structure of an Italian Slum*, (University of Chicago Press, 1958).

3. Robert Golding, William Golding, and Edmund L. Epstein, *Lord of the Flies*, (Follettbound, 2002).

4. Rutger Bregman, "The Real Lord of the Flies: What Happened When Six Boys Were Shipwrecked for 15 Months," *The Guardian*, January 6, 2021, https://www.theguardian.com/books/2020/may/09/the-real-lord-of-the-flies-what-happened-when-six-boys-were-shipwrecked-for-15-months.

5. Joe C. Magee and Adam D. Galinsky, "Social Hierarchy: The Self-Reinforcing Nature of Power and Status," *The Academy of Management Annals* 2, no. 1 (January 2008): 351–398.

6. Cameron Anderson and Gavin J. Kilduff, "The Pursuit of Status in Social Groups," *Current Directions in Psychological Science* 18, no. 5 (October 2009): 295–298.

7. "Presidential Candidates Debate," *C-Span*, October 17, 2000, https://www.c-span.org/video/?159297-1/presidential-candidates-debate, 10:35-10:45. Accessed April 11, 2024.

8. FastTheLatestNews, "Famous Debate Moment Gore Intrudes Bush's Personal Space in 2000," Video, *YouTube*, July 14, 2013, https://www.youtube.com/watch?v=cn4Z2r8I2Pw. Accessed 14 March 2024.

9. Chris Lipp and Antoine De Morree, *Magnetic: How Great Leaders Persuade and Inspire* (Kendall/Hunt Publishing Company, 2021).

10. Jay A. Conger, "The Necessary Art of Persuasion," *Harvard Business Review*, April 4, 2023, https://hbr.org/1998/05/the-necessary-art-of-persuasion.

11. David Dubois, Derek D. Rucker, and Adam D. Galinsky, "Dynamics of Communicator and Audience Power: The Persuasiveness of Competence versus Warmth," *Journal of Consumer Research* 43, no. 1 (February 22, 2016): 68–85.

12. Joe C. Magee and Adam D. Galinsky, "Social Hierarchy: The Self-Reinforcing Nature of Power and Status," *The Academy of Management Annals* 2, no. 1 (January 2008): 351–398.

13. Joe C Magee, "From action to power: the use of action-orientation in inferences of power," (PhD diss., Stanford University, 2004).

14. George W. Bush, "2000 Victory Speech," *American Rhetoric*, December 13, 2000, https://www.americanrhetoric.com/speeches/gwbush2000victoryspeech.htm.

15. Peter M. Gollwitzer, "Implementation Intentions: Strong Effects of Simple Plans," *American Psychologist* 54, no. 7 (July 1999).

16. Corinne Bendersky and Neha Shah, "The Cost of Status Enhancement: Performance Effects of Individuals' Status Mobility in Task Groups," *Organization Science* 23, no. 2 (April 2012): 308–322.

17. Charlie L. Hardy and Mark Van Vugt, "Nice Guys Finish First: The Competitive Altruism Hypothesis," *Personality and Social Psychology Bulletin* 32, no. 10 (October 2006): 1402–1413.

18. Jorge Moll et al., "Human Fronto–Mesolimbic Networks Guide Decisions about Charitable Donation," *Proceedings of the National Academy of Sciences of the United States of America* 103, no. 42 (October 2006): 15623–15628.

19. Robert Iger, *The Ride of a Lifetime: Lessons Learned from 15 Years as CEO of the Walt Disney Company* (Random House, 2019).

20. Cristina M. Gomes and Christophe Boesch, "Wild Chimpanzees Exchange Meat for Sex on a Long-Term Basis," *PLoS One* 4, no. 4 (2009).

21. Cameron Anderson and Gavin J. Kilduff, "The Pursuit of Status in Social Groups," Current *Directions in Psychological Science* 18, no. 5 (October 2009): 295–298.

22. Leah Silverman, "Robbers Cave Experiment: The Psychological Study Of Unsupervised Boys That Inspired *Lord of the Flies*," *All That's Interesting*, November 7, 2023, https://allthatsinteresting.com/robbers-cave-experiment. Accessed 15 March 2024.

23. Saul Mcleod PhD, "Robbers Cave Experiment | Realistic Conflict Theory," *Simply Psychology*, September 27, 2023, https://www.simplypsychology.org/robbers-cave.html. Accessed 15 March 2024.

24. Adam D. Galinsky, Deborah H. Gruenfeld, and Joe C. Magee, "From Power to Action," *Journal of Personality and Social Psychology* 85, no. 3 (January 2003): 453–466.
25. Joris Lammers et al., "Power Gets the Job: Priming Power Improves Interview Outcomes," *Journal of Experimental Social Psychology* 49, no. 4 (July 1, 2013): 776–779.

Additional Reading

Serena Chen, Annette Y. Lee-Chai, and John A. Bargh, "Relationship Orientation as a Moderator of the Effects of Social Power," *Journal of Personality and Social Psychology* 80, no. 2 (January 2001): 173–187.

Francis J. Flynn et al., "Helping One's Way to the Top: Self-Monitors Achieve Status by Helping Others and Knowing Who Helps Whom," *Journal of Personality and Social Psychology* 91, no. 6 (January 2006): 1123–1137.

Michael Schaerer et al., "Advice Giving: A Subtle Pathway to Power," *Personality and Social Psychology Bulletin* 44, no. 5 (January 2018): 746–761.

Leigh Plunkett Tost, Francesca Gino, and Richard P. Larrick, "Power, Competitiveness, and Advice Taking: Why the Powerful Don't Listen," *Organizational Behavior and Human Decision Processes* 117, no. 1 (January 2012): 53–65.

Xueguang Zhou, "The Institutional Logic of Occupational Prestige Ranking: Reconceptualization and Reanalyses," *American Journal of Sociology* 111, no. 1 (July 2005): 90–140.

Chapter 4

1. TBN, "Rick Warren (The Purpose Driven Life): Understand & Accept God's Love | Praise on TBN," Video, *YouTube*, May 19, 2021, https://www.youtube.com/watch?v=ZneXln1UtS8. Accessed 15 March 2024.

2. Maya M. Kuehn, Serena Chen, and Amie M. Gordon, "Having a Thicker Skin," *Social Psychological and Personality Science* 6, no. 6 (April 2015).

3. "Address to Joint Session of Congress May 25, 1961," John F. Kennedy Presidential Library and Museum, n.d., https://www.jfklibrary.org/learn/about-jfk/historic-speeches/address-to-joint-session-of-congress-may-25-1961. Accessed 15 March 2024.

4. Chip Heath and Dan Heath, *Made to Stick: Why Some Ideas Survive and Others Die* (Random House, 2007).

5. Grant Packard and Jonah Berger, "How Concrete Language Shapes Customer Satisfaction," *Journal of Consumer Research* 47, no. 5 (July 2020): 787–806.

6. Pamela K. Smith and Yaacov Trope, "You Focus on the Forest When You're in Charge of the Trees: Power Priming and Abstract Information Processing," *Journal of Personality and Social Psychology* 90, no. 4 (2006): 578–596.

7. Cheryl J. Wakslak, Pamela K. Smith, and Albert Han, "Using Abstract Language Signals Power.," *Journal of Personality and Social Psychology* 107, no. 1 (January 2014): 41–55.

8. NPR, "Transcript of Barack Obama's Victory Speech," NPR, November 5, 2008, https://www.npr.org/2008/11/05/96624326/transcript-of-barack-obamas-victory-speech. Accessed 15 March 2024.

9. Tim Fernholz, "What It Took for Elon Musk's SpaceX to Disrupt Boeing, Leapfrog NASA, and Become a Serious Space Company," *Quartz*, July 21, 2022, https://qz.com/281619/what-it-took-for-elon-musks-spacex-to-disrupt-boeing-leapfrog-nasa-and-become-a-serious-space-company.

10. TBN, "Rick Warren (The Purpose Driven Life): Understand & Accept God's Love | FULL EPISODE | Praise on TBN," Video, YouTube, May 19, 2021, 34:02 to 34:07, https://www.youtube.com/watch?v=ZneXln1UtS8. Accessed 15 March 2024.

11. Ibid., 38:23
12. Ibid., 41:40
13. "1932 United States Presidential Election," *Wikipedia*, February 15, 2024, https://en.wikipedia.org/wiki/1932_United_States_presidential_election. Accessed 15 March 2024.
14. Michael E. Eidenmuller, "Franklin Delano Roosevelt - Commonwealth Club Address," n.d., https://www.americanrhetoric.com/speeches/fdrcommonwealth.htm. Accessed 15 March 2024.
15. David E. Hamilton, "Herbert Hoover: Campaigns and Elections," Miller Center, October 4, 2016, https://millercenter.org/president/hoover/campaigns-and-elections.
16. "1980 United States Presidential Election," *Wikipedia*, February 19, 2024, https://en.wikipedia.org/wiki/1980_United_States_presidential_election. Accessed 15 March 2024.
17. "Ronald Reagan 1980 Presidential Campaign," *Wikipedia*, December 7, 2023, https://en.wikipedia.org/wiki/Ronald_Reagan_1980_presidential_campaign. Accessed 15 March 2024.
18. Kimberly Amadeo, "Obama 2008 Economic Promises and Platform," *The Balance*, February 24, 2021, https://www.thebalancemoney.com/obama-2008-economic-promises-and-platform-3305774.
19. Malik Simba, "'Yes We Can': Barack Obama's Road to the White House, 2008," December 10, 2020, https://www.blackpast.org/african-american-history/yes-we-can-barack-obamas-road-white-house-2008. Accessed 15 March 2024.
20. Linda Smircich and Gareth Morgan, "Leadership: The Management of Meaning," *The Journal of Applied Behavioral Science* 18, no. 3 (September 1982): 257–273.
21. "Why We're Behind – Will We Catch Up?," *The Voyage – Special Section* (April 24, 1961): 29.

22. "Address to Joint Session of Congress May 25, 1961," John F. Kennedy Presidential Library and Museum, n.d., https://www.jfklibrary.org/learn/about-jfk/historic-speeches/address-to-joint-session-of-congress-may-25-1961. Accessed 15 March 2024.

23. Obama Foundation, "Author Dave Eggers in Conversation with President Barack Obama," Video, *YouTube*, November 20, 2018, 22:15 to 22:36, https://www.youtube.com/watch?v=N7ZHDoNhScY. Accessed 15 March 2024.

24. Robert J. Baum, Edwin A. Locke, and Shelley A. Kirkpatrick, "A Longitudinal Study of the Relation of Vision and Vision Communication to Venture Growth in Entrepreneurial Firms," *Journal of Applied Psychology* 83, no. 1 (1998): 43–54.

25. Jobs official, "Steve Jobs Brainstorms with the NeXT Team 1985 | Jobs Official," Video, *YouTube*, November 23, 2017, https://www.youtube.com/watch?v=Udi0rk3jZYM. Accessed 15 March 2024.

26. Simon Sinek, "How Great Leaders Inspire Action," Video, *TED Talks*, n.d., https://www.ted.com/talks/simon_sinek_how_great_leaders_inspire_action. Accessed 15 March 2024.

27. "Mike McCue," *Wikipedia*, December 22, 2023, https://en.wikipedia.org/wiki/Mike_McCue. Accessed 15 March 2024.

28. TechCrunch, "(Founder Stories) Mike McCue: The TellMe Years," Video, *YouTube*, June 9, 2011, https://www.youtube.com/watch?v=rcmTTDA3aLQ. Accessed 15 March 2024.

29. Yair Berson et al., "Leading from Different Psychological Distances: A Construal-Level Perspective on Vision Communication, Goal Setting, and Follower Motivation," *The Leadership Quarterly* 26, no. 2 (April 2015): 146.

30. Nira Liberman and Yaacov Trope, "The Role of Feasibility and Desirability Considerations in near and Distant Future Decisions: A Test of Temporal Construal Theory." *Journal of Personality and Social Psychology* 75, no. 1 (1998): 5.

31. Laura Huang et al., "Sizing up Entrepreneurial Potential: Gender Differences in Communication and Investor Perceptions of Long-Term Growth and Scalability," *Academy of Management Journal* 64, no. 3 (June 2021): 716–740.

32. Priyanka D. Joshi et al., "Gender Differences in Communicative Abstraction," *Journal of Personality and Social Psychology* 118, no. 3 (March 2020): 417–435.

33. Elinor Amit, Shai Danziger, and Pamela K Smith, "Medium is a Powerful Message: Pictures Signal less Power than Words," *Organizational Behavior and Human Decision Processes* 169 (February 2022).

34. "The Twelve Steps | Alcoholics Anonymous," n.d., https://www.aa.org/the-twelve-steps. Accessed 15 March 2024.

35. Marc Medina, "The Paradox of Self-Surrender and Self-Empowerment: An Investigation of the Individual's Understanding of the Higher Power in Alcoholics Anonymous," *Counselling Psychology Review* 29, no. 3 (September 2014): 28–42.

36. Ibid., 39.

37. Lisa Rosequist, *The Experience of Surrender: For Women with Non-Metastatic Breast Cancer Undergoing a Psychospiritual Integration and Transformation (PSIT) Intervention.* Institute of Transpersonal Psychology, 2009.

38. Timothy Patrick Blanco, "The Concept of a Higher Power and Control Orientation Among Recovering Alcoholics." PhD diss., (Fielding Graduate Institute, 2003).

39. Ibid., 92.

40. Stanford University, "'You've Got to Find What You Love,' Jobs Says" *Stanford News*, August 24, 2022, https://news.stanford.edu/2005/06/12/youve-got-find-love-jobs-says.

41. Chris Lipp, "6 Rules to Win TechCrunch Disrupt," *Speak Value*, January 14, 2022, https://speakvalue.com/6-rules-to-win-techcrunch-disrupt. Accessed 15 March 2024.

42. Antonio L. Freitas, Peter M. Gollwitzer, and Yaacov Trope, "The Influence of Abstract and Concrete Mindsets on Anticipating and Guiding Others' Self-Regulatory Efforts," *Journal of Experimental Social Psychology* 40, no. 6 (November 2004): 739–752.

43. Pamela K. Smith, Daniel H.J. Wigboldus, and Ap Dijksterhuis, "Abstract Thinking Increases One's Sense of Power," *Journal of Experimental Social Psychology* 44, no. 2 (March 2008): 378–385.

Additional Reading

Sarah J. Gervais et al., "Power Increases Situated Creativity," *Social Influence* 8, no. 4 (October 2013): 294–311.

Chapter 5

1. Stephen Silver, "25 Years Ago, Apple's Board of Directors Pushed Out CEO John Sculley," *AppleInsider,* June 18, 2018, https://appleinsider.com/articles/18/06/18/25-years-ago-apples-board-of-directors-pushed-out-ceo-john-sculley.

2. Benjamin Mayo, "Scott Forstall Was Fired from Apple 10 Years Ago Today," *9to5Mac*, October 29, 2022, https://9to5mac.com/2022/10/29/scott-forstall-apple-decade.

3. David A. Owens, "Negotiating Order in R&D Groups: A Model of Status Dynamics in Groups and Organizations," PhD diss. (Stanford University, 1998).

4. Jobs official, "Steve Jobs Brainstorms with the NeXT Team 1985 | Jobs Official," Video, *YouTube*, November 23, 2017,

https://www.youtube.com/watch?v=Udi0rk3jZYM. Accessed 15 March 2024.

5. David A. Owens, "Negotiating Order in R&D Groups: A Model of Status Dynamics in Groups and Organizations," PhD diss. (Stanford University, 1998): 63.

6. Dave Smith, "Apple Has a New Global-Supply-Chain Boss – This Anecdote about How He Handled a Meeting with Tim Cook Shows Why He's the Perfect Man for the Job," *Business Insider*, July 1, 2019, https://www.businessinsider.com/apple-promotes-sabih-khan-svp-operations-tim-cook-china-story-2019-6.

7. David A. Owens, "Negotiating Order in R&D Groups: A Model of Status Dynamics in Groups and Organizations," PhD diss. (Stanford University, 1998).

8. Kirsten M. Keller, "Power Conflict: Struggles for Intragroup Control and Dominance," PhD diss., (University of Maryland, 2009).

9. David A. Owens, "Negotiating Order in R&D Groups: A Model of Status Dynamics in Groups and Organizations," PhD diss. (Stanford University, 1998).

10. Hee Young Kim, Nathan C. Pettit, and Laura Reitman, "Status Moves: Evaluations and Effectiveness of Status Behaviors," *Group Processes & Intergroup Relations* 22, no. 1 (July 2017): 139–159.

11. Lawrence G. Shattuck, "Communicating Intent and Imparting Presence," *Military Review* (March-April 2000): 66–72.

12. Ana Guinote, "How Power Affects People: Activating, Wanting, and Goal Seeking," *Annual Review of Psychology* 68, no. 1 (January 2017): 353–381.

13. C. Shawn Burke et al., "Trust in Leadership: A Multi-Level Review and Integration," *The Leadership Quarterly* 18, no. 6 (December 2007): 606–632.

14. Cat Clifford, "Whole Foods CEO John Mackey: How to 'Devastate Employee Morale' in a Single Blow," *CNBC*, November 12, 2020, https://www.cnbc.com/2020/11/11/whole-foods-ceo-john-mackey-ho.html.

15. Yidan Yin, Krishna Savani, and Pamela K. Smith, "Power Increases Perceptions of Others' Choices, Leading People to Blame Others More," *Social Psychological and Personality Science* 13, no. 1 (January 2022): 170–177.

16. Corinne Bendersky and Nicholas A. Hays, "Status Conflict in Groups," *Organization Science* 23, no. 2 (April 2012): 323–40.

17. Peter H. Kim, Robin L. Pinkley, and Alison R. Fragale, "Power Dynamics in Negotiation," *Academy of Management Review* 30, no. 4 (October 2005): 799–822.

18. Adam D. Galinsky, Deborah H. Gruenfeld, and Joe C. Magee, "From Power to Action," *Journal of Personality and Social Psychology* 85, no. 3 (January 2003): 453–466.

Additional Reading

Steven L. Blader and Yaru Chen, "Differentiating the Effects of Status and Power: A Justice Perspective," *Journal of Personality and Social Psychology* 102, no. 5 (January 2012): 994–1014.

Lindred L. Greer and Corinne Bendersky, "Power and Status in Conflict and Negotiation Research: Introduction to the Special Issue," *Negotiation and Conflict Management Research* 6, no. 4 (October 2013): 239–252.

Lindred L. Greer and Gerben A. Van Kleef, "Equality versus Differentiation: The Effects of Power Dispersion on Group Interaction," *Journal of Applied Psychology* 95, no. 6 (January 2010): 1032–1044.

Boris Groysberg, Jeffrey T. Polzer, and Hillary Anger Elfenbein, "Too Many Cooks Spoil the Broth: How High-Status Individuals Decrease Group Effectiveness," *Organization Science* 22, no. 3 (June 2011): 722–737.

Christine L. Porath, Jennifer R. Overbeck, and Christine M. Pearson, "Picking up the Gauntlet: How Individuals Respond to Status Challenges," *Journal of Applied Social Psychology* 38, no. 7 (June 2008): 1945–1980.

Beth H. Richardson et al., "The Cooperation Link: Power and Context Moderate Verbal Mimicry," *Journal of Experimental Psychology: Applied* 25, no. 1 (March 2019): 62–76.

Chapter 6

1. Stanford GSB Staff, "Margaret Neale: Why You Should Make the First Move in a Negotiation," *Stanford Graduate School of Business*, February 13, 2024, https://www.gsb .stanford.edu/insights/margaret-neale-why-you-should-make-first-move-negotiation.

2. Michael W. Morris and Dacher Keltner, "How Emotions Work: The Social Functions of Emotional Expression in Negotiations," *Research in Organizational Behavior* 22 (January 2000): 1–50.

3. The Adelante Movement, "How Sheryl Sandberg Negotiated Her Facebook Deal," Video, *YouTube*, January 17, 2015, 00:16 to 00:20, https://www.youtube.com/watch?v=jlaWONj MIAs. Accessed 15 March 2024.

4. Ibid., 02:16 to 02:30.

5. Ruolei Gu et al., "Be Strong Enough to Say No: Self-Affirmation Increases Rejection to Unfair Offers," *Frontiers in Psychology* 7 (November 2016).

6. David A. Owens, "Negotiating Order in R&D Groups: A Model of Status Dynamics in Groups and Organizations," PhD diss. (Stanford University, 1998).

7. Christian Thuderoz, "Why Do We Respond to a Concession With Another Concession? Reciprocity and Compromise," *Negotiation Journal* 33, no. 1 (January 2017): 71–83.

8. Darren Hardy, "How to Handle Disrespect," Video, *YouTube*, July 2023, https://www.youtube.com/watch?v=bhoXZtQZw4c.

9. Dominic Nicholls, "Ukrainian Peace Negotiators 'Unprepared' for KGB Tactics of Russia's Bully Boys," *The Telegraph*, March 22, 2022, https://www.telegraph.co.uk/world-news/2022/03/22/ukrainian-peace-negotiators-unprepared-russias-aggressive-kgb.

10. Stanford Graduate School of Business, "Conducting Effective Negotiations," Video, *YouTube*, July 28, 2009, https://www.youtube.com/watch?v=rCmvMDrCWjs. Accessed 15 March 2024.

11. David A. Owens, "Structure and Status in Design Teams: Implications for Design Management," *Design Management Journal Academic Review*, 2000, p. 59.

12. John C. Georgesen and Monica J. Harris, "The Balance of Power: Interpersonal Consequences of Differential Power and Expectancies," *Personality and Social Psychology Bulletin* 26, no. 10 (November 2000): 1239–1257.

13. John T. Copeland, "Prophecies of Power: Motivational Implications of Social Power for Behavioral Confirmation," *Journal of Personality and Social Psychology* 67, no. 2 (August 1994): 264–277.

14. Jean Louise Kahwajy, "Toward a Theory of Social Receiving: Effects of Target Openness and Modifiability on Expectancy Confirmation Processes," PhD diss., (Stanford University, 2000).

15. BBC News, "FULL Interview: Prince Harry and Meghan Markle - BBC News," Video, *YouTube*, November 27, 2017, https://www.youtube.com/watch?v=LQicq60aJaw. Accessed 15 March 2024.

16. Emily T. Amanatullah, Michael W. Morris, and Jared R. Curhan, "Negotiators Who Give Too Much: Unmitigated Communion, Relational Anxieties, and Economic Costs

in Distributive and Integrative Bargaining," *Journal of Personality and Social Psychology* 95, no. 3 (September 2008): 723–738.

17. Alice Chen, Council Member of The City of Stafford, TX, October 2022.

18. Derek D. Rucker, Adam D. Galinsky, and David Dubois, "Power and Consumer Behavior: How Power Shapes Who and What Consumers Value," *Journal of Consumer Psychology* 22, no. 3 (July 2011): 352–368.

19. "Dandamis," *Wikipedia*, January 7, 2024, https://en .wikipedia.org/wiki/Dandamis#:~:text=When%20 Onescratus%20encountered%20Dandamis%20in,in%20 his%20bed%20of%20leaves. Accessed 15 March 2024.

20. Julie Bort, "Amazon Founder Jeff Bezos Explains Why He Sends Single Character '?' Emails," *Inc.Com*, January 5, 2021, https://www.inc.com/business-insider/amazon-founder-ceo-jeff-bezos-customer-emails-forward-managers-fix-issues.html.

21. Vanessa M. Patrick and Henrik Hagtvedt, "How to Say 'No': Conviction and Identity Attributions in Persuasive Refusal," *International Journal of Research in Marketing* 29, no. 4 (December 2012): 390–394.

22. Vanessa Patrick, *The Power of Saying No: The New Science of How to Say No That Puts You in Charge of Your Life* (Sourcebooks, 2023): 87.

23. "Loss Aversion," *Wikipedia*, February 20, 2024, https:// en.wikipedia.org/wiki/Loss_aversion. Accessed 15 March 2024.

24. Burak Oc, Michael R. Bashshur, and Celia Moore, "Speaking Truth to Power: The Effect of Candid Feedback on How Individuals with Power Allocate Resources," *Journal of Applied Psychology* 100, no. 2, (March 2015): 450–463.

25. Vanessa Patrick, *The Power of Saying No: The New Science of How to Say No That Puts You in Charge of Your Life* (Sourcebooks, 2023): 87.
26. Michael E. McCullough et al., "Interpersonal Forgiving in Close Relationships: II. Theoretical Elaboration and Measurement," *Journal of Personality and Social Psychology* 75, no. 6 (December 1998): 1586–1603.
27. Karl Aquino, Thomas M. Tripp, and Robert J. Bies, "Getting Even or Moving on? Power, Procedural Justice, and Types of Offense as Predictors of Revenge, Forgiveness, Reconciliation, and Avoidance in Organizations," *Journal of Applied Psychology* 91, no. 3 (May 2006): 653–668.

Additional Reading

Wei Cai and Song Wu, "Powerful People Feel Less Fear of Negative Evaluation," *Social Psychology* 48, no. 2 (March 2017): 85–91.

Serena Chen, Jordan A. Tharp, and Maya M. Kuehn, "They Love Me, They Love Me Not?: Social Power Shapes Expectations of Acceptance and Concerns about Rejection," *Social Cognition* 35, no. 5 (October 2017): 563–584.

Deborah C. Zetik and Alice F. Stuhlmacher, "Goal Setting and Negotiation Performance: A Meta-Analysis," *Group Processes & Intergroup Relations* 5, no. 1 (January 2002): 35–52.

Chapter 7

1. Brett Martin, "Postmortem of a Venture-Backed Startup," *Medium*, June 17, 2020, https://medium.com/@brett1211/postmortem-of-a-venture-backed-startup-72c6f8bec7df.
2. Alix Spiegel, "She Offered the Robber a Glass of Wine, and That Flipped the Script," *NPR*, July 15, 2016, https://www.npr.org/sections/health-shots/2016/07/15/485843453/it-was-a-mellow-summer-dinner-party-then-the-gunman-appeared.

3. Adam D. Galinsky et al., "Power Reduces the Press of the Situation: Implications for Creativity, Conformity, and Dissonance," *Journal of Personality and Social Psychology* 95, no. 6 (January 2008): 1450–1466.

4. Robert Rosenthal and Donald B. Rubin, "Interpersonal Expectancy Effects: The First 345 Studies," *Behavioral and Brain Sciences* 1, no. 3 (September 1978): 377–386.

5. John C. Georgesen and Monica J. Harris, "The Balance of Power: Interpersonal Consequences of Differential Power and Expectancies," *Personality and Social Psychology Bulletin* 26, no. 10 (November 2000): 1239–1257.

6. Nathaniel Branden, *Nathaniel Brandens Self-Esteem Every Day: Reflections on Self-Esteem and Spirituality* (Simon and Schuster, 1998): 173.

7. Pablo Briñol et al., "The Effects of Message Recipients' Power before and after Persuasion: A Self-Validation Analysis." *Journal of Personality and Social Psychology* 93, no. 6 (December 2007): 1040–1053.

8. Annika Scholl and Kai Sassenberg, "Where Could We Stand If I Had…? How Social Power Impacts Counterfactual Thinking after Failure," *Journal of Experimental Social Psychology* 53 (July 2014): 51–61.

9. Dacher Keltner, Deborah H. Gruenfeld, and Cameron Anderson, "Power, Approach, and Inhibition," *Psychological Review* 110, no. 2 (April 2003): 265–284.

10. Pablo Briñol, Richard E. Petty, and Benjamin Wagner, "Body Posture Effects on Self-evaluation: A Self-validation Approach," *European Journal of Social Psychology* 39, no. 6 (August 2009): 1053–1064.

11. Nathanael J. Fast and Serena Chen, "When the Boss Feels Inadequate," *Psychological Science* 20, no. 11 (November 2009): 1406–1413.

12. John T. Copeland, "Prophecies of Power: Motivational Implications of Social Power for Behavioral Confirmation," *Journal of Personality and Social Psychology* 67, no. 2 (August 1994): 264–77.

13. Ana Guinote, "How Power Affects People: Activating, Wanting, and Goal Seeking," *Annual Review of Psychology* 68, no. 1 (January 2017): 353–381.

14. Jean Louise Kahwajy, "Toward a Theory of Social Receiving: Effects of Target Openness and Modifiability on Expectancy Confirmation Processes," PhD diss., (Stanford University, 2000): 42.

15. Cameron Anderson, Oliver P. John, and Dacher Keltner, "The Personal Sense of Power," *Journal of Personality* 80, no. 2 (February 2012): 313–344.

16. John T. Copeland, "Prophecies of Power: Motivational Implications of Social Power for Behavioral Confirmation," *Journal of Personality and Social Psychology* 67, no. 2 (August 1994): 264–277.

17. Gün R. Semin and Klaus Fiedler, "The Cognitive Functions of Linguistic Categories in Describing Persons: Social Cognition and Language," *Journal of Personality and Social Psychology* 54, no. 4 (April 1988): 558–568.

18. Sonia K. Kang et al., "Power Affects Performance When the Pressure Is On," *Personality and Social Psychology Bulletin* 41, no. 5 (April 2015): 726–735.

19. "Interviewing Workshop and Panel Discussion," *Genentech, Association for Women in Science*, April 11, 2015.

20. Andreas Jäger, David D. Loschelder, and Malte Friese, "How Self-Regulation Helps to Master Negotiation Challenges: An Overview, Integration, and Outlook," *European Review of Social Psychology* 26, no. 1 (January 2015): 203–246.

21. Elizabeth Nieto, "Diversity and Inclusion at Work," *eCornell*, February 21, 2024.

22. Ted Koppel, "Nightline," *ABC News*, June 21, 1990, 28:45 to 33:07, https://www.youtube.com/watch?v=ryO3En-zG68. Accessed 15 March 2024.

23. Michael W. Kraus, Serena Chen, and Dacher Keltner, "The Power to Be Me: Power Elevates Self-Concept Consistency and Authenticity," *Journal of Experimental Social Psychology* 47, no. 5 (September 2011): 974–980.

24. C. Nathan DeWall et al., "How Leaders Self-Regulate Their Task Performance: Evidence That Power Promotes Diligence, Depletion, and Disdain," *Journal of Personality and Social Psychology* 100, No. 1 (January 2011): 47-65.

25. Shuang Wu, Rachel Smallman, and Pamela K. Smith, "Self-Control Signals and Affords Power," *Journal of Personality and Social Psychology* (January 2024).

26. Stanford Graduate School of Business, "Oprah Winfrey on Career, Life, and Leadership," Video, *YouTube*, April 28, 2014, 24:55 to 24:59, https://www.youtube.com/watch?v=6DlrqeWrczs. Accessed 15 March 2024.

27. Olivier Klein and Mark Snyder, "Stereotypes and Behavioral Confirmation: From Interpersonal to Intergroup Perspectives," *Advances in Experimental Social Psychology* 35 (2003): 153–234.

28. Russell H. Fazio, Edwin A. Effrein, and Victoria J. Falender, "Self-Perceptions Following Social Interaction," *Journal of Personality and Social Psychology* 41, no. 2 (August 1981): 232–242.

29. Geoffrey L. Cohen et al., "Reducing the Racial Achievement Gap: A Social-Psychological Intervention," *Science* 313, no. 5791 (September 2006): 1307–1310.

30. Alan Moorehead, *Gallipoli* (Aurum, 2015).

31. Sonia K. Kang et al., "Power Affects Performance When the Pressure Is On," *Personality and Social Psychology Bulletin* 41, no. 5 (April 2015): 726–735.

32. Piotr Oleś and Hubert J. M. Hermans, "Allport-Vernon Study of Values," *The Corsini Encyclopedia of Psychology*, January 2010, 1–2.

33. Jean Louise Kahwajy, "Toward a Theory of Social Receiving: Effects of Target Openness and Modifiability on Expectancy Confirmation Processes," PhD diss., (Stanford University, 2000).

Additional Reading

Jeff C. Brodscholl, Hedy Kober, and E. Tory Higgins, "Strategies of Self-regulation in Goal Attainment versus Goal Maintenance," *European Journal of Social Psychology* 37, no. 4 (September 2006): 628–648.

Carsten K.W. De Dreu and Gerben A.Van Kleef, "The Influence of Power on the Information Search, Impression Formation, and Demands in Negotiation," *Journal of Experimental Social Psychology* 40, no. 3 (May 2004): 303–319.

John C. Georgesen and Monica J. Harris, "Why's My Boss Always Holding Me down? A Meta-Analysis of Power Effects on Performance Evaluations," *Personality and Social Psychology Review* 2, no. 3 (August 1998): 184–195.

Deborah H. Gruenfeld et al., "Power and the Objectification of Social Targets," *Journal of Personality and Social Psychology* 95, no. 1 (January 2008): 111–127.

Li Huang et al., "Powerful Postures versus Powerful Roles," *Psychological Science* 22, no. 1 (December 2010): 95–102.

Traci Mann, Denise De Ridder, and Kentaro Fujita, "Self-Regulation of Health Behavior: Social Psychological Approaches to Goal Setting and Goal Striving," *Health Psychology* 32, no. 5 (January 2013): 487–498.

Dongwon Min and Kim Ji-Hern, "Is Power Powerful? Power, Confidence, and Goal Pursuit," *International Journal of Research in Marketing* 30, no. 3 (September 2013): 265–275.

Bogdan Wojciszke and Anna Struzynska-Kujalowicz, "Power Influences Self–Esteem," *Social Cognition* 25, no. 4 (August 2007): 472–494.

Shuang Wu, Rachel Smallman, and Pamela K. Smith, "Self-Control Signals and Affords Power," *Journal of Personality and Social Psychology* (January 2024).

Chapter 8

1. Adam D. Galinsky, Derek D. Rucker, and Joe C. Magee, "Power: Past Findings, Present Considerations, and Future Directions," in *APA Handbook of Personality and Social Psychology, Vol. 3. Interpersonal Relations*, eds. Mario Mikulincer and Phillip R. Shaver (Washington, DC: American Psychological Association, 2015), p. 421–460.

2. Cameron Anderson and Gavin J. Kilduff, "Why Do Dominant Personalities Attain Influence in Face-to-Face Groups? The Competence-Signaling Effects of Trait Dominance," *Journal of Personality and Social Psychology* 96, no. 2 (January 2009): 491–503.

3. Corinne Bendersky and Neha Shah, "The Downfall of Extraverts and Rise of Neurotics: The Dynamic Process of Status Allocation in Task Groups," *Academy of Management Journal* 56, no. 2 (April 2013): 387–406.

4. Vassilia Binensztok @DrVassilia, May 23, 2021, https://twitter.com/DrVassilia/status/1396479203541934086. Accessed 15 March 2024.

5. Muping Gan, Daniel Heller, and Serena Chen, "The Power in Being Yourself: Feeling Authentic Enhances the Sense of Power," *Personality and Social Psychology Bulletin* 44, no. 10 (May 2018): 1460–1472.

6. Cameron Anderson and Jennifer L. Berdahl, "The Experience of Power: Examining the Effects of Power on Approach and Inhibition Tendencies," *Journal of Personality and Social Psychology* 83, no. 6 (January 2002): 1362–1377.

7. Ana Guinote, "How Power Affects People: Activating, Wanting, and Goal Seeking," *Annual Review of Psychology* 68, no. 1 (January 2017): 353–381.

8. Ana Guinote, "Power Affects Basic Cognition: Increased Attentional Inhibition and Flexibility," *Journal of Experimental Social Psychology* 43, no. 5 (September 2007): 685–697.

9. Brené Brown, "Brené Brown on What Vulnerability Isn't," Feb 23, 2021, in *ReThinking*, podcast with Adam Grant, 32:08 to 32:28, https://link.chtbl.com/wV1wfiX7.

10. Larissa Z. Tiedens, "Anger and Advancement versus Sadness and Subjugation: The Effect of Negative Emotion Expressions on Social Status Conferral," *Journal of Personality and Social Psychology* 80, no. 1 (January 2001): 86–94.

11. Charles S. Carver and Eddie Harmon-Jones, "Anger is an Approach-Related Affect: Evidence and Implications," *Psychological Bulletin* 135, no. 2 (March 2009): 183–204.

12. Andreas Jäger, David D. Loschelder, and Malte Friese, "How Self-Regulation Helps to Master Negotiation Challenges: An Overview, Integration, and Outlook," *European Review of Social Psychology* 26, no. 1 (January 2015): 203–246.

13. Bonnie E. Erickson et al., "Speech Style and Impression Formation in a Court Setting: The Effects of 'Powerful' and 'Powerless' Speech," *Journal of Experimental Social Psychology* 14, no. 3 (May 1978): 266–279.

14. Ana Guinote, "Power and Goal Pursuit," *Personality and Social Psychology Bulletin* 33, no. 8 (June 2007): 1076–1087.

15. Martha Jeong et al., "Communicating with Warmth in Distributive Negotiations Is Surprisingly Counterproductive," *Management Science* 65, no. 12 (December 2019): 5813–5837.

16. David A. Owens, "Negotiating Order in R&D Groups: A Model of Status Dynamics in Groups and Organizations," PhD diss. (Stanford University, 1998).

17. Mike Hofman, "Young Bill Gates Was an Angry Office Bully," GQ, October 28, 2015, https://www.gq.com/story/young-bill-gates-was-an-angry-office-bully.

18. Joel Spolsky, "My First BillG Review," *Joel on Software*, December 5, 2016, https://www.joelonsoftware.com/2006/06/16/my-first-billg-review.

19. Joey T. Cheng, Jessica L. Tracy, and Joseph Henrich, "Pride, Personality, and the Evolutionary Foundations of Human

Social Status," *Evolution and Human Behavior* 31, no. 5 (September 2010): 334–347.

20. Hee Young Kim, Nathan C. Pettit, and Laura Reitman, "Status Moves: Evaluations and Effectiveness of Status Behaviors," *Group Processes & Intergroup Relations* 22, no. 1 (July 2017): 139–159.

21. Dacher Keltner, Deborah H. Gruenfeld, and Cameron Anderson, "Power, Approach, and Inhibition," *Psychological Review* 110, no. 2 (April 2003): 265–284.

22. Rainer Zitelmann, "Bill Gates Was an Angry, Difficult Boss in Early Microsoft Days—Here's Why Employees Still Liked Him," *CNBC*, February 24, 2020, https://www .cnbc.com/2020/02/24/bill-gates-was-difficult-boss-in-early-microsoft-days-but-employees-still-liked-him.html.

23. Richard C. Savin-Williams, "Dominance in a Human Adolescent Group," *Animal Behaviour* 25 (May 1977): 400–406.

24. Hee Young Kim, Nathan C. Pettit, and Laura Reitman, "Status Moves: Evaluations and Effectiveness of Status Behaviors," *Group Processes & Intergroup Relations* 22, no. 1 (July 2017): 139–159.

25. LinkedIn News, "Bill Gates on Maximizing Joy and Changing as a Leader - Career Advice from Some of the Biggest Names in Business," Video, *LinkedIn*, December 18, 2018, https://www.linkedin.com/learning/career-advice-from-some-of-the-biggest-names-in-business/bill-gates-on-maximizing-joy-and-changing-as-a-leader. Accessed 15 March 2024.

26. David A. Owens, "Negotiating Order in R&D Groups: A Model of Status Dynamics in Groups and Organizations," PhD diss. (Stanford University, 1998).

27. Cameron Anderson, Oliver P. John, and Dacher Keltner, "The Personal Sense of Power," *Journal of Personality* 80, no. 2 (February 2012): 313–344.

28. Peter Belmi and Jeffrey Pfeffer, "Power and Death: Mortality Salience Increases Power Seeking While Feeling Powerful Reduces Death Anxiety," *Journal of Applied Psychology* 101, no. 5 (January 2016): 702–720.
29. Yona Kifer et al., "The Good Life of the Powerful," *Psychological Science* 24, no. 3 (January 2013): 280–288.
30. Dacher Keltner, Deborah H. Gruenfeld, and Cameron Anderson, "Power, Approach, and Inhibition," *Psychological Review* 110, no. 2 (April 2003): 271.
31. Lisa H. Nishii, "Fostering an Inclusive Climate," *eCornell*, February 25, 2024.
32. Stanford Graduate School of Business, "Oprah Winfrey on Career, Life, and Leadership," Video, *YouTube*, April 28, 2014, https://www.youtube.com/watch?v=6DlrqeWrczs. Accessed 15 March 2024.
33. Julie Spencer-Rodgers et al., "The Power of Affirming Group Values: Group Affirmation Buffers the Self-Esteem of Women Exposed to Blatant Sexism," *Self and Identity* 15, no. 4 (February 2016): 419.
34. Ibid., 422.

Additional Reading

Daniel R. Ames and Francis J. Flynn, "What Breaks a Leader: The Curvilinear Relation between Assertiveness and Leadership," *Journal of Personality and Social Psychology* 92, no. 2 (February 2007): 307–324.

Jeanne M. Brett et al., "Sticks and Stones: Language, Face, and Online Dispute Resolution," *Academy of Management Journal* 50, no. 1 (February 2007): 85–99.

Pablo Briñol et al., "Power and Persuasion: Processes by Which Perceived Power Can Influence Evaluative Judgments," *Review of General Psychology* 21, no. 3 (September 2017): 223–241.

Dana R. Carney, Judith A. Hall, and Lavonia Smith LeBeau, "Beliefs about the Nonverbal Expression of Social Power," *Journal of Nonverbal Behavior* 29, no. 2 (June 2005): 105–123.

Nathanael J. Fast et al., "Power and Overconfident Decision-Making," *Organizational Behavior and Human Decision Processes* 117, no. 2 (March 2012): 249–260.

Judith A. Hall, Erik J. Coats, and Lavonia Smith LeBeau, "Nonverbal Behavior and the Vertical Dimension of Social Relations: A Meta-Analysis," *Psychological Bulletin* 131, no. 6 (January 2005): 898–924.

Robert G. Lord, Christy L. De Vader, and George M. Alliger, "A Meta-Analysis of the Relation between Personality Traits and Leadership Perceptions: An Application of Validity Generalization Procedures," *Journal of Applied Psychology* 71, no. 3 (August 1986): 402–410.

Priscilla S. Rogers and Song Mei Lee-Wong, "Reconceptualizing Politeness to Accommodate Dynamic Tensions in Subordinate-to-Superior Reporting," *Journal of Business and Technical Communication* 17, no. 4 (October 2003): 379–412.

Robert I. Sutton and Andrew Hargadon, "Brainstorming Groups in Context: Effectiveness in a Product Design Firm," *Administrative Science Quarterly* 41, no. 4 (December 1996): 685.

Zachary Witkower et al., "Two Signals of Social Rank: Prestige and Dominance Are Associated with Distinct Nonverbal Displays," *Journal of Personality and Social Psychology* 118, no. 1 (January 2020): 89–120.

Chapter 9

1. Alexandra L. Decker et al., "Striatal and Behavioral Responses to Reward Vary by Socioeconomic Status in Adolescents," MIT Libraries, January 22, 2024, https://dspace.mit.edu/handle/1721.1/153394. Accessed 15 March 2024.

2. Lisa H. Nishii, "Fostering an Inclusive Climate," *eCornell*, February 25, 2024.

3. Nathanael J. Fast et al., "Illusory Control," *Psychological Science* 20, no. 4 (April, 2009): 502–508.

4. "Sermon on the Mount," n.d., https://blessedare.org/sermon. Accessed 15 March 2024.

About the Author

Chris Lipp, M. A. is a professor of management communication at Tulane University and author of three books on pitching, persuasion, and power. His book, *The Startup Pitch*, became the first book to outline the complete formula found in successful investment pitches. Chris spends time as an international pitch coach helping startups secure venture capital, and his coaching has contributed to raising hundreds of millions of dollars. Chris' second book, *Magnetic*, provides a systematic way to apply persuasion across communication. Chris trained thousands of individuals in his corporate workshops at organizations like Google and Microsoft to communicate for impact. Chris previously taught management communication at Rice University and University of Southern California. At Stanford, he co-founded *Stanford Leaders in Communication*, a program that supported graduate students in using persuasion skills to effect change at local and statewide policy levels.

Index